MW00772437

The Way To Get Over A Breakup

How to Get Past Your Breakup in Style and Recover Like The Queen You Are

Ellie K. Flores

Seven Suns Book Press

CONTENTS

BONUS BOOK

How to Discover and Confront Infidelity in Your Relationship

Unravels the many warning signs a cheating partner displays, and discovers how to confirm those suspicions, and confronts them with evidence.

(Download at www.littlebookhut.com)

INTRODUCTION

Bad breakup? Tell me about it!

But it was supposed to last forever, no? You had finally found your soul mate, or so you thought. But then what happened? Things started to fall apart. And one day, you found yourself all alone in the apartment you got for yourselves to start a new phase of life, eating ice cream straight out of the tub, and watching Gilmore Girls. You found yourself helpless with tasks that he had taken responsibility for. You couldn't find your focus, your attention span grew shorter, and you felt out of place. Some days, you couldn't stop eating and on others, you'd have difficulty swallowing a bite.

It's crazy, isn't it? You feel like burning the whole world because everything feels unfair. You feel betrayed, cheated, and taken advantage of. You had only heard about how much it pains to lose someone you love. But you never knew you would have to go through the pain yourself.

I have been there too. Like you, I was heartbroken. Every cell of my body ached in a way that I never thought it would. And the worst part: no one could understand what I was going through. No one understood why I couldn't get out of bed in the morning, carry on with day-to-day tasks like a "normal" person, or just get over it. Ah, that last bit hits different, doesn't it? Isn't it so easy to tell someone to just get over it?

Like, hey, why didn't I think of it before? Why didn't I just "get over it"? Absurd, I tell you!

But after a few days, the very same idea started to grow on me. It does make sense to get over it, doesn't it? Why would I want to waste any more time than I already did on a man who didn't value me? Who disregarded every opinion I had? Why did I think he deserved any more of my time or tears?

You see, relationships are like the Carolina Reaper—the hottest pepper in the world. As you bite in, its fruity and sweet flavor sends you to all the good places you can think of. Those first days of romance and courtship, the shyness and hesitation in taking things forward, holding hands, kissing under the mistletoe on the coldest nights of December, and just being in love—ahh, nothing tops that. The memories themselves serve as a reminder of the glorious days you lived.

But as you bite in some more, that's when all hell breaks loose. The sweet and fruitiness turn bitter, and unbearable pain, the kind you have never known before and wouldn't wish upon your enemies, churns your stomach. Every breath you take, the agony increases. Every breath reminds you of the mistake you made. It might have started as a bet for a vlog with some friends, but only you can know the hot chili hell you are in.

No amount of sweetness can cut through the heat that's embedded in every nerve in your tongue. I know this because I have been in this situation once. I have tried a Carolina Reaper and been in a relationship too, and both memories are not so great to recall.

Some people believe that you have to go through heartbreak to know real love. I don't agree. Real love shouldn't hurt. It shouldn't leave you feeling rejected, vulnerable, and in immense pain. You can't talk about how much it hurts because others don't get it. They think you will take a few weeks to get over it. But does the foul taste in your mouth ever go? Do you ever forget who you were when with that special person your world once centered around?

A breakup is the death of a relationship. The ultimate end. But unlike most endings, it can be a new beginning too. A beginning, where you learn about yourself, love yourself and get over a boy who didn't have the guts to keep you his forever. Breakups are hard. Some are messy too. Some happen before you even realize it. Some are sudden, and some take forever.

When a breakup happens, even if you knew it would, the world comes crashing down on you. You fail to recall a life without them. You fail to remember who you were as a person. You try to salvage it, get over it in stupid ways like going for a rebound, isolating yourself from friends and family, binge eating, etc., but remember that this phase—this ugly phase where you don't feel like going to work and want to stay in your jammies all day—will pass, and time will heal. There are many things you can do to come out stronger and happier from a failed relationship.

It takes guts, resilience, and courage to get over it. Speaking from personal experience, going through a breakup is a difficult and laborious phase. You need to acknowledge what went wrong, why it went wrong, and what not to do in the coming relationships. It calls for a deep self-analysis where you try to rebuild yourself from scratch, rediscover who you are without your partner, and learn to love yourself. Why? Simply because, as women, we are told to be selfless. We are labeled givers. We think from our hearts. We find goodness in everyone else. This often leads to ending up in toxic relationships that add no value to our lives. In the end, we are left with nothing for ourselves, hopelessness, and guilt. When a partner parts ways, we feel unattractive, at fault, and emotional. We lose all confidence in ourselves and suffer from poor self-esteem. How will we ever find someone to love again, we constantly ask ourselves. In the worst of cases, to rebalance our sense of self, we hook up with the wrong guys and date men who are nothing like our definition of a perfect man, all because we feel secondhand.

But we aren't hand-me-downs. We are young, strong, confident women who deserve to be loved every minute of the day.

With this goal in mind, let's collect our thoughts, push hard and move forward. Let's learn how to gracefully carry ourselves through this difficult time, not give in to the impulses of pursuing another man right away, and come out of the current mess we are in.

It might have happened yesterday, a week from today, or a few months ago... it doesn't matter where you are on the journey right now. What truly matters is how to get out of that state of helplessness, unkindness, and disappointment that you feel in yourself.

And the best part: do it in style. I want you to do it like the queen you are. I want you to forget about the nastiness and turn over a new leaf.

That guy didn't deserve the wholesomeness that you are. In fact, he couldn't deal with it.

Together, let's regain our lost confidence, rediscover love, and rebuild our self-worth. Let's be our best selves, compassionate and kind. Let's be empathetic and rise again with courage, confidence, and a strong sense of self-worth.

PART I

I Just Broke Up with My Man

It had been several days since Nina had that odd lump in her throat. She had this gut feeling that something wasn't right. Was Jake taking too much stress about his new job? What was it that he wasn't telling her? Was moving in with him a hasty decision? But they had known each other for over seven months now. It seemed like the right thing to do. Was she wrong?

Such thoughts never left her mind. He would come home late every night and then rush to get in bed and sleep after dinner. There was no intimacy between them. He had always been the one who wanted to get frisky right after getting home, but no such impulsiveness had been initiated by him in recent times. Nina called her sister, a happily married woman with two toddler twins. Her advice: if he isn't getting intimate, you take charge. She knew that Jake loved surprises. She decided to doll up one day and take him out for lunch. Only when she went to his office, she learned that he never made it. Shocked and worried that something awful happened to him in the morning, Nina called him. Casually asked him how his day was going. He, being unaware of her being in his office, told her that he was busy delivering a pitch to his boss in the conference room and apologized that he couldn't talk right now.

Was he lying? But why?

"Does he often come in late?" she asked the receptionist.

"Yes. He usually comes in with his boss in her car."

But he took his car every day to work, sharp at seven. Nina came home, didn't tell him that she had visited him today, and decided to follow him after he left home tomorrow. To her surprise, he parked his car at his boss's house and stayed some good two hours with her. Nina stayed in the car, unable to process what could bring him here this early. After a while, she saw both of them stepping out of the house, giggling and touching each other like newlyweds who couldn't get enough of each other.

Tears started to roll down. All the work she had put into the relationship, how she had fought with her parents who didn't approve of him, how she turned a blind eye to all the comments from her friends that Jake was being flirty with them... This is how he repaid her. By cheating on her with his boss.

The truth hit her like a bolt. Not in her wildest dreams would Nina have thought that this would happen to her. She had never experienced heartbreak before. Jake was her first-ever boyfriend and in her mind, surely the last. She had done everything right. She was supportive of his career choices. She happily took care of his needs inside the house. From grocery shopping to going to her parents on holidays, she never bothered Jake if he didn't want to go.

Then why her?

OUCH, IT HURTS

IF YOU HAVE EVER been heartbroken, you know the amount of pain you experience the first few days. There is no end to your tears. Every thought begins and ends with your ex in it. You keep calling them, messaging them, trying to salvage something that isn't salvageable. You wake up feeling disheartened and unmotivated and go to bed feeling even more broken. It's like someone has stolen your peace of mind. You don't want to get out of bed or reply back to messages from your friends and family worrying about your mental and emotional state. You don't bother doing the laundry, the kitchen sink is full of unwashed dishes, and you are eating junk straight out of the packet.

These are pretty common symptoms everyone experiences after a breakup. It doesn't matter who pulled the plug. A breakup leaves a plethora of emotions you alone have to deal with.

It's acceptable because we are talking about someone you could have given your life for. It's hurtful when the person you wanted to spend your future with no longer wants to be a part of it. Now that they have left, the world expects you to get on with life as if nothing happened.

The moments right after a breakup are the hardest to endure. You can't think right, act right, or make sense of things. Your "forever love" ended all ties with you, in a brutal and hurtful manner. It's fair that you feel lost and in pain.

Mourning a breakup is a lot like mourning someone that passed away. They are no longer a part of your everyday life, but they aren't bothered with how you are or who you are with. It doesn't matter to them if you are well or unwell, moving on or feeling stagnant, or know how to live on without them. They don't care. They are gone, gone for good.

During the first few weeks, you may go through various stages of separation. If the breakup wasn't mutual and came as a shocking revelation, the first stage, of course, is denial. You don't want to accept that something so terrible and heart-wrenching happened to you. You don't know how to process it either. You want to stay cuddled up in a blanket, shutting off every thought that comes in your head. This is both painful and difficult.

Next comes depression where you go into a deep sadness that can last many days or weeks. During this phase, you just breathe your way through life, not live it. Days become longer and so do the nights. Nothing subdues the pain you feel.

Passing that phase is unbearable for many, which is when they try to mend ties with their ex. You might find yourself texting or calling your ex and begging them to take you back. Stop. Don't beg. You deserve better.

If he had cared for you, he would have thought about you before going out and cheating behind your back. If he valued your presence in his life, he would have tried to make things work. If he felt like falling out of love, he would have made the effort to rekindle the spark in one way or another. But he chose the easy way out. He chose to cut you out of his life and move on with someone more intriguing. He valued his freedom and free will over you. Do you really want to have him back after the way he treated you?

What naturally comes after that realization is anger and frustration.

How dare he, you ask yourself. How could he have chosen someone else when you did everything in your power to keep him happy? How could he not value the sacrifices you made for him so that he can pursue his dreams peacefully?

How could he forget how you gave up an amazing opportunity to move states but he wanted to be close to his mama? How could he forget that you gave up music lessons because he thought you should both save some money? How could he ignore the fact that you chose him above many others, who by the way, would have made you happier, much happier?

It's appalling, right?

Once that anger subdues, comes acceptance—the most beautiful and hopeful part of the journey. Acceptance enables you to free yourself from any guilt you feel, any shame you associated with the end of the relationship, and all negativity you had within you. Through acceptance, you begin to put in the work and rebuild. You pick up the pieces and mend yourself. You realize that you deserve better. You relearn your worth and value. You relearn how to love yourself and make yourself a priority in your life. You regain your confidence and self-esteem.

EFFECTS OF A BAD BREAKUP

BELIEVE IT OR NOT, a breakup post-relationship drains you both emotionally and physically. We have often heard people tell someone to get over their ex already. But there are reasons why it is so difficult for some of us to just move on with our lives and forget that we ever shared a life with someone else. I'll tell you exactly why.

When you enter a relationship with a partner, you make some promises to each other. You commit yourself to being with them. Your days begin and end with them in it. Your daily lives, activities, and routines overlap. It's always someone's turn to use the bathroom first because the other partner takes too long. Chores are divided. Meals and activities are planned according to one's availability and schedule. Date nights require dressing up. Going to events as a couple takes prep too. In a way, you feel like one.

Now imagine you wake up one day and nothing goes as per routine. Your shared identity as a couple disappears. You come from an empty home to an empty bed. You have to do the things they did, yourself. You have no one to share inside jokes with or watch a movie on Netflix with.

According to a series of studies related to relationships and breakups, researchers found that people after a breakup are left bewildered (Cosier, 2010). They lose their sense of identity. Since they have molded themselves into someone their partner adored, they no longer remember who they were as a person themselves.

Second, heartbreaks don't just hurt the heart metaphorically. Heartache hurts just as much as any physical pain. The brain reacts to heartbreak in the same way it does to any physical injury.

One study aimed to test this theory in 2011 and used brain imaging to record the activity of the brain of people who suffered a breakup recently (Kross et al., 2011). During the experiment, researchers showed the participants images of their exes. Their brain's response was monitored. Then, they were exposed to painful levels of heat. Their brain activity was again recorded. Surprisingly, both experiments had the same level of effect on the brain, confirming that emotional loss is not less than physical pain.

So don't try to avoid the pain. Let it hurt you. Let it make you stronger. Let it help you recover. Let it become a memory of the past.

Then, there is the psychological effect of breakups too. According to David Sbarra, a professor of clinical psychology, breakups affect our attachment systems. Attachment systems refer to strong bonds we form with the people we live our lives with. These include primary caregivers, educators, friends, and partners. As we mature in adulthood, we attach to our romantic partners. Our partners keep our physical systems in balance. They help set routines, offer a shoulder to cry on when we are sad, help us deal with our anger when we feel frustrated, and energize us whenever we lag. They are our security blanket—the people who we rely on to keep us afloat in life. When a breakup happens, this attachment breaks. This connection is lost. This can lead to you feeling helpless and lost.

In association with that, your biological rhythm also changes. When you enter a new relationship, it doesn't take long for both partners to form habits that complement each other. Your body knows when it's time to eat, sleep, and relax. Your mind and body become one. So when a breakup happens, everything goes haywire. Your body and mind lose their sense of connection with your partner. Without warning, you are forced to find a way to operate both mentally and physically on your own.

Not to mention, losing a partner is like losing an investment too. All the people in our lives are long-term investments. There is a give-and-take relationship in between. We expect certain things from people and they expect something in return too. A long-term relationship is an investment that, upon a breakup, goes to waste. You lose several years of your life, your prime years, while dating someone. You make compromises and sacrifices for them. You put in the effort to keep it smooth and strong. You spend your time, energy, and emotion on this person. You plan your future with them. Your world revolves around them. And then comes a hard slap on your face in the form of a breakup that brings you back to reality.

Besides, some long-term partners become so addicted to their partners that when a split happens, they are forcibly dragged out of their euphoric, blissful state.

POST–BREAKUP: WHAT MUST YOU DO?

SINCE A BREAKUP CAN take this level of a toll on your mental, emotional, and physical health, the first thing you need is to be kind to yourself. Who else will look after you if you won't? You must understand that your body goes into a state of shock when the breakup comes out of nowhere. One day you are cuddling someone, imagining your future, and talking to them, and the next day they come to you wanting an out. The loss is real. The grief should be too. The loss will make you scared and lonely because it comes unexpectedly. The body wishes to recover but it doesn't know how.

Therefore, start by being compassionate and empathetic toward yourself. Give yourself the same treatment you would give to a friend who is going through the same.

You wouldn't ask her to shut down emotionally or never leave the house. Instead, you would encourage her to show strength, forget about her ex, and forgive herself because there is no reason for her to blame herself.

Post-breakup, especially during the first 30 days after the breakup, the goal shouldn't be to stay distracted and spend time doing meaningless things. The goal should be to mourn so that you begin the process of healing. Healing happens when you acknowledge and label the emotions you feel. It happens when you feel ready to release yourself from those emotions that bring pain. Healing happens when you accept that your relationship with your partner has ended and ended for good.

Wanting to distract yourself is considered avoidance. The more you delay and avoid confronting how you feel, the longer it will take you to recover. Since you want to do it like a queen, you better follow these four things on the list for the first 30 days post-breakup.

Stay away from your ex's social media. Block him from every means of communication you had with them or else you will soon find yourself texting or calling him a week or two from now. The fewer reminders of your ex in your life, the better. It doesn't matter if you called it quits with him—guilt and loneliness can make us do crazy things. I don't want you to fall into their trap and delay moving forward. Stalking your ex is one of the most fascinating and obvious things you may do. You want to know how he is doing, what he is doing, and who he is doing it with. You want to see karma hit him for breaking up. But don't. Stay away from being tempted to scroll his socials or keep tabs on him.

According to one study, exes who keep tabs on their former partners have negative feelings for them (Marshall, 2012). Despite that, they are more likely to try to contact them, desire to be with them, and, therefore, less likely to heal and move forward.

Second, get rid of his stuff. If you had been living together, chances are many things belong to your ex in your previously shared space. For both of you to move forward, you need to get rid of the stuff that reminds you of each other. For an emotional cleanse, a house cleanse is a must! Remove every trace of him from your personal space. Return all gifts, souvenirs you kept of special dates, and things he paid for like an appliance or TV. Within the first week of the split, pack his stuff in a box and put it away. If he wishes to come back to take it, good. If he doesn't, mail it to him so that it's out of your hair. This will further encourage moving on and cultivate acceptance in you.

Delete any pictures or videos of the two of you from your phone and laptop. Keeping his images on your phone will involuntarily make you see him. The memories associated with those pictures will only remind you more of him. It's going to be difficult to do so but as soon as you hit Delete All, there will be no going back. Grieving will become a lot less painful when you don't have anything to associate your ex with.

Avoid mentioning him in conversations with friends, colleagues, or family. Sometimes, it's easier to let go when your ex's name doesn't come up in conversations. Mentioning his name will bring back the memories you two shared. It will only confuse your heart and make you do stupid things like calling him and asking for a meet-up or casual hangout. If he hurt you, he needs to be forgotten—simple as that!

Avoid emotional triggers. Emotional triggers bring up a strong memory of your relationship and stick to the mind. There will be days when you miss him the most. If you had been together for months or years, chances are that you celebrated many festivals and holidays with him. So keep in mind that these holidays are going to leave you pestered. I suggest you plan in advance to keep yourself busy around that time. Take up things you normally wouldn't so that you remain occupied. Keep busy, plan a trip with friends, visit your family, or volunteer somewhere. If you let emotional triggers get to you, you will be back to square one. All the progress you have made so far will go down the drain. Apart from remembering the good ol' days, you will have to relive the trauma of the breakup too.

I AM AN EMOTIONAL MESS

THERE IS A LOT of misconception about how long it takes you to recover from heartbreak. If you still find yourself crying or reminiscing about the past with your ex, no need to stress yourself out. There is no timeline you need to follow. Everyone heals differently. Some take more time and some don't. The goal here is to allow yourself to feel ready to move on, not do it because everyone around you tells you to.

But when will you recover? Many factors will determine that. Every situation is different. Every relationship is different. The reasoning behind every breakup is different. So you can't measure it with some scale of expectancy. Only you know how you are feeling. Only you know how far you still need to go. Only you can tell whether you have healed or not.

Some factors, as we talked about earlier, include the following:

Who left who: Who dumped who? If he left you, it might take longer for you to move on. If you left them, then there was a little part of you already planning an escape before it actually happened. So you already began healing and prioritizing yourself over your relationship before he knew it. Thus, the healing may happen sooner than you think.

How long you two were together: How long did the relationship last? How many memories have you created together? How many birthdays, festivals, vacations, and anniversaries have you celebrated together? The longer you two were together, the harder it will be to get over it.

Were you two on the same page?: Sometimes, one partner is more involved and invested in the relationship than the other. When a breakup happens, they are bound to feel more hurt, no matter who called it quits. Their investment meant more commitment, more sacrifices, and more attention. Most of the time, it is us women because we can't stop giving.

Infidelity: If infidelity caused the breakup, there is nothing more shocking than that revelation, in whatever form it comes. You are left feeling unwanted, wronged, and cheated on. You feel insecure, abandoned, and unlovable.

You lose trust in love and assume that every other relationship will be this hurtful.

These factors can determine the amount of time you need to recover from the breakup. Just remember, getting over your ex will become easier when you throw the rules out of the window. Know that there will come a time when you will feel your best, refreshed, and unburdened. You will feel alive, confident, and ready to fall in love again. Recovery is imminent. So don't lose heart if you feel better one day and worse the next. Like some medicine, healing makes you feel worse in the beginning and then better.

My advice: don't feel pressured. Don't listen to how others healed. Your journey is your own.

BAWLING YOUR EYES OUT IS IMPORTANT

FOR HEALING TO HAPPEN naturally, you need to grieve your loss first. Losing someone in today's day and time is harder than you think. You are so connected through mutual friends, social media, and family that it's hard to break all ties. Somewhere, someone just reminds you of your ex, and all hell breaks loose. Apart from mentioning the ex in casual conversations, people can be as hurtful as expecting you to forget about it as if it never happened. It doesn't make sense to them why you are still in mourning. Friends would expect you to show up with another date when they host parties for couples because inviting you solo doesn't seem like an option. They will try to hook you up with other people despite you not being ready for it.

After the first few weeks of counseling and support, that's when people really start to show who they are. They will stop empathizing with you, seem uninterested in your stories, stop checking up on you, or help you with day-to-day chores. That's when the true realization of being alone really hits. You are expected to go back to living your normal life and pick up pieces of your heart, glue them back, and give them to someone else.

But it isn't a movie, is it?

I know you are a queen, but even queens need their time to heal from a painful experience. When they get wounded on battlefields, shielding their people, they too need some time to recover and go back. So why is it not the same for you? You may not have physical wounds on display, but you are equally hurting—actually more because there are no scars to measure how well or poorly you are doing.

So cry. Ugly cry.

Cry your heart out. Whenever you feel like it. Cry when in bed and upon waking up. Let those feelings out of your system. Keeping it all in is a sign of avoidance. You can't deny or fake your well-being. You need to be okay to feel okay. Healing begins when you acknowledge how you feel. Healing begins when you allow yourself to mourn. Crying provides a release like nothing else. It makes you feel lighter than before.

It improves your mood and helps you recover in a shorter time (Gračanin et al., 2014). In *Crying: The Mystery of Tears*, author William H. Frey talks about how crying releases high levels of cortisol, the stress hormone. You basically wash out everything that worries you about your past, present, and future through crying. This not only allows for an emotional cleanse but also makes you feel so much better (Frey & Langseth, 1985). Crying acts as a natural antidepressant because it boosts your mood and is self-soothing. One study revealed the same results as when one takes an antidepressant to calm their anxiety, feel less depressed, and relieve stress (Rottenberg et al., 2008). Think of it as a free-of-cost mood-boosting medicine.

Crying your eyes out also bursts your bubble of fantasy. Crying brings you back to reality to face your worries. Once you are done, you feel more awakened; things start to make sense, and your perspective changes. You feel calmer than when you had it all bottled up. Clarity of mind is an instrumental gift that comes with crying. Mourning what you once loved gives you a chance to make peace with your present and hope for a better future. This doesn't mean that you stop feeling sad; rather it means that you are one step closer to facing your new reality. For once, you can see your ex as a human as opposed to a scumbag. You can realize that people aren't perfect. He wasn't either. Also, his loss!

Finally, by crying, you acknowledge that you are wounded. You acknowledge that you need some space and time off to feel better again. You prioritize your feelings above all. You allow yourself to grieve. You empower yourself to let those painful memories wash over you.

That's when letting go of your ex becomes easier.

Acknowledgment of your feelings and emotions after a bad breakup empowers you to make peace with them. It happened. There is nothing you can do now to reverse it. What's left then? Moving forward. That's what you need to look forward to. You aren't dependent on that loser of a man anymore. You can bid him goodbye and move forward. That chapter is forever closed now. All you need is to jumpstart healing. Yes, the more important phase of your life right now.

Healing is what will help you see things from a clearer perspective. It will help you look at yourself in the mirror again and see that pretty smile across your lips. It is what will take away every ounce of sadness and guilt from your system and fill it with hope, positivity, and thoughts about a better, more promising, enriching future.

Crying for days and weeks is counterproductive because you then feel stuck. You need to learn to let go of all the painful reminders and cleanse your soul and mind of your ex's memory. To do that, you need to learn the art of forgiveness.

LETTING GO: FORGIVENESS COMES IN ALL SHAPES AND SIZES

BUDDY ARISTOTLE PUTS LOVE in such a cute manner. According to him, our true nature is to love and be loved. But this seems like the last thing on your mind when you experience heartbreak. If it were in your nature to love and be loved, why are you single? Why aren't you married off to the love of your life and bringing new life into this world? Doesn't that sound like the way of things?

More importantly, how can you love someone who hurts you? How can you think about being in love again when you have just gone through a breakup? How can it be in your nature to forgive and forget something so easily and so soon?

They say forgiveness is a gift you present yourself. This means that it should come wrapped up in shiny wrapping paper or be snuck under a Christmas tree, waiting to be opened, right? In a hypothetical world, it just might!

However, since the whole idea is about accepting your reality, forgiveness does have its perks. It is something that promises closure, positivity, and hope of moving forward. It may come off as a terrifying idea to forgive your ex who broke your heart but it is also important if you wish to ever fall in love again. You see, many of us move forth in relationships without having forgiven our exes. What happens next is that we compare our current partners to our ex. We can't trust anything they say or do. There is little trust. You don't feel genuine with your feelings about them. You keep trying to recreate the memories you made with your ex.

In short, your mind becomes stuck. Maybe that's why people call it a gift you give yourself. Perhaps that's what it truly means. You free yourself from anything painful. You free yourself from any guilt or shame you feel. You acknowledge that you have been hurt but are also ready to take the risk of falling in love again. With forgiveness, you take control of your life and stop being a victim.

Forgiveness doesn't mean you are weak. It means that you no longer hold a grudge against them. It means that you no longer care about how they are, what they are doing, or who they are with.

Forgiveness means letting go of the emotional baggage you carry on your shoulders all the time. Forgiveness means that you are ready to accept that your ex wasn't perfect. It means giving yourself and your future partner a chance that you both deserve to be happy. With forgiveness, there is no recycled anger. Through forgiveness, you opt for a life where you hold the reins of your horse. You move it at your desired pace with your head held high and shoulders confident. Your unresolved anger, resentment, and bitterness no longer dominate you.

Many confuse forgiveness with letting your ex off the hook. It doesn't mean you forget what happened. It simply means that you are ready to overlook it for your own sanity and heal.

Forgiveness means telling yourself that we are all good and loving souls but occasionally get lost. This doesn't mean that you try to justify your ex's cheating but rather recognize that people hurt others sometimes. They do so from a place of limited thinking or because they experienced hurt in their past too.

Forgiveness is reminding yourself that you aren't perfect either. It's about remembering your own mistakes and others forgiving you over them. It involves opening your heart and mind to being optimistic about people without holding grudges or harboring resentments.

Forgiveness means taking back control of your emotions. When you hold onto negative thoughts about someone, you give them the chance to control your mood and emotions. Why? Why would you want to give anyone but yourself that power over your emotional and mental state?

Finally, remember that when people respond to hate from a place of hate, anger to anger, they are a part of the problem cycle. They become who they despise because they do the same things. It starts a challenge of who does it worse. When this happens, there is only one way you go and that is downhill.

So how can you forgive your ex when the pain is still fresh and raw? How can you move on without feeling vulnerable for doing so? How can you improve your chances of finding a happier, more optimistic self within yourself through forgiveness?

Write a letter to your ex, explaining all the grudges and resentments you have against him. Pour your heart out until no tear is left within the eye. Repair what's damaged by letting it all out. You don't have to mail it to them.

Gain awareness of the emotions that arise when you think about your ex. Think about three to five ways his memories affect you. Doing so will be less painful in the future when you recall this past relationship because you will be well aware of your triggers and how they affect you. You can also devise counteractive plans to handle these emotions.

Seek help and support from your friends and family. Have them hear your story. Sometimes, all you need is to vent out and unburden yourself. Talking to a close friend can facilitate the process.

Be generous toward yourself. The best way to release yourself from any guilt or pain is by being compassionate toward yourself. Remind yourself frequently, using positive affirmations and confidence-lifting mantras, that you deserve the best of the world. Remind yourself how letting go of the pain is the only way to heal. Keeping it all in won't do you any good or your ex any bad.

Be accountable. Take responsibility for how your actions and behaviors gave rise to any conflicts or disputes. Two people are responsible for the dynamics of a healthy relationship. If you are to blame for some of the mess that led to bigger messes, take responsibility for it. There shouldn't be any shame in doing so as no one will judge you. This will only improve your chances of knowing your triggers and hopefully, prevent the same mistakes again.

Don't let wounds fester. If you continue to hold grudges, you will never break the vicious chain of negativity. You will never break free of it if you have self-defeating thoughts. Challenge your thoughts and beliefs and process what happened. Keep the big picture in mind where you end up with someone deserving of you, who loves and cherishes you.

Besides, how can you forget that being awesome and happy with your newfound freedom is the best revenge there can be? There is nothing better than putting your energies and time into doing what you love and with whom you love it. Get busy in life by pursuing the dreams you left behind and goals you gave up because of your ex. Once you learn to fall in love with your wholesomeness again, your ex will be a thing of the past—*literally!*

When you have grieved your loss and forgiven your ex, it means you have decided to move forward. As much as I want you to do that right away and forget all about your ex's wrongdoings and hurt, there is something that you must consider. What happened? Why did he break up with you? If you called it quits, why did you?

Knowing what went wrong and why is also an imperative step before you go seeking out a new love. You need to realize your priorities in a relationship so that you don't end up making the same mistakes with another partner.

It is both easy and comforting to just pass on the blame to someone else and take no responsibility. But what if you had an equal part in the separation? You may have compelled him to go somewhere else without knowing. You may have pushed him away, emotionally shut him down, or simply gotten busy and distanced. Could that be the reason why he went out to seek love from somewhere else?

This may come off as a serious accusation but think about it. Why did he break up with you? Or why couldn't you love him anymore?

What Really Happened?

THERE CAN BE A hundred reasons for the breakup, not just one. It's easy to call someone a cheater or dominant in a relationship when there are so many layers to uncover. Why men cheat has a whole science to it. Why they like to dominate women and think of them as lesser is another science altogether.

In my opinion, it has a lot to do with the conditioning one receives from early childhood. In countries where divorce rates are higher and it's easy to replace one partner with another, cheating is a common norm. Go back a few decades and you will find women being sold into marriage in exchange for a certain number of sheep. The prettier the woman, the more her value. They had to dress up like play dolls to be desired. They had little to no say in who they wished to marry. Any courtship that didn't end in marriage was blamed on the woman being undesirable. She would then have a harder time finding another man because the rumors spread fast.

Similar but different conditioning can be observed in women who have been taught to be people pleasers. They have been taught they must give up their hobbies, interests, and dreams and prioritize a man. They are expected to cook, clean, and look after their partners like mothers and nannies.

It isn't hard to understand the implications of such a narrative. Men become more confident and dominant in their demands whereas women become more giving, caring, and selfless.

Why relationships don't last forever has a lot to do with this type of thinking. Before we talk about some much-needed introspection, let's understand how people-pleasing leads to many unhealthy choices women make in relationships.

THE PARADOX OF PEOPLE-PLEASING

WHO IS A GOOD woman? Someone worthy of being valued, cherished, and taken care of? Is it someone who says yes to everything? Is it someone who happily gives up her career and manages the house? Is it someone who keeps her opinions to herself and stays in the kitchen where she belongs? Is it someone who always says yes to sex even when she doesn't want to? Is a good woman a combination of all these things?

Umm, no!

As women, we are surrounded by societal pressures of being nurturers, caregivers, and mothers. Don't look any further than your own mother to see how true this is. Neglecting and sacrificing her needs for the sake of her spouse and children is an in-built quality. This toxic stereotyping of roles where the man earns and the women are seen as homemakers, despite working the same job, bogs down women all around the globe and compels them to let go of their careers, dreams, and aspirations because they have domestic duties to fulfill.

In this pursuit of being the best girlfriend, wife, and mother, we lose our identities all because we have been taught to please others. People-pleasing is a learned behavior where you seek others' approval to feel valuable and positive about yourself. You fear that if you don't conform to the norms of society it will disown you from it. You do it to seek approval and validation. You do the same when you are in a relationship. You give more to your relationship than your partner because it somehow confirms your worth or value.

People-pleasing does play a crucial role in how women approach and view relationships. When women are conditioned to think that everything they do that upsets their man is their fault, they can never become equal partners in a relationship. This is one reason why we never rise up to manipulation and tell our partners how they try to dominate us. This is one reason we keep killing our dreams so that our men can fulfill theirs. This is why we let abuse and exploitation drill us into being good women when people-pleasing is the very trait we need to unlearn.

Remember, people-pleasing isn't a goodwill gesture. It tells your partner that you are willing to go the extra mile every time he falls short of his promises. It tells him that you are ready to sacrifice your needs and wants and make theirs your priority.

Luckily, people-pleasing is a learned norm and, therefore, can be unlearned. However, it requires conscious effort and action. You need to learn to put yourself first, express your opinions, and take responsibility for your dreams and aspirations. You need to stop seeking validation from your partner or anyone related to him. You need to stop ignoring your emotional needs at the expense of someone else's happiness. You need to stop being generous when the person in front of you brings nothing to the relationship.

You can break free from the compartmentalization society puts you in. Yes, you can demand equal rights, appreciation, and ownership of your decisions in your relationships. You should.

Otherwise, men will keep taking advantage of you and blame you for being a bad woman. They will keep playing you like a harp on the tune they choose to play.

The reason I want you to take charge is so that you can make wiser decisions about who to date the next time. The anger you feel right now is not because your partner cheated on you. It is partially because you allowed it to happen. Even if you called it quits, you know you should have done it a long time ago. Yet, you let it go on, hoping for a miracle to change how he treated you.

Build a more secure sense of self-worth and attachment style so you know what you are looking for in a relationship.

Coming back to understanding what went wrong and why the breakup happened, let's decode the most common reasons your relationship didn't work. Chances are, you already know many of these, yet you still fell for them.

WHY DID IT END?

WE EACH HAVE OUR reasons for either breaking up or staying together in a relationship. We all have unique challenges that come up from time to time. The key to success is how these issues are handled. Some partners are quick to address them while others let them fester until they become the reason for a breakup.

In your case, you must know what went wrong and why you ended up breaking up or being dumped. Why did the relationship not work out? What issues were left unaddressed? Why weren't they addressed promptly? If your partner ended up cheating, what made him do it? If you fell out of love with him, what behaviors led to it?

All these are important questions to understand what role you played in the breakup. The revelations might be shocking and painful, but you need to tackle them. You need the knowledge to avoid making the same mistakes again with another partner, or worse, fall for the same traps you did the first time. The more information you have, the more equipped and in control you will be in all your relationships. Not to mention, you will heal faster when you come to terms with what happened and what you could have done differently.

Were there trust issues? Did you or your partner have insecurities about one another? Was he overly possessive of you? Did he check your messages and ask you who you called during the day? Did he keep asking you about every guy that looked at you at a restaurant or in a grocery store?

Lack of trust in relationships is one of the most common reasons why couples grow apart. Trust issues give rise to other problems like jealousy, aggressiveness, possessiveness, emotional and sexual infidelity, etc. The constant checking-in and not believing what the other person is telling can get on one's nerves easily. They may feel trapped and untrustworthy because their partner believes so.

Were you two on two different pages about the future? Did he want you to quit your job and move with him to where he worked? Did he expect you to become a stay-at-home partner/mother to your children? Did he expect you to cater to his family 24/7?

Understandably, different people might have different versions of how they see themselves in the future. However, when the ideas clash on a level where there is no in-between to compromise on, couples fall apart. After the honeymoon phase ends and the realities of life hit, many couples realize that their expectations from one another aren't similar.

Was communication always a problem? Was it all about his needs, his dreams, and his aspirations? Did you feel like there was a lack of proper communication? Did you feel like your needs were unmet and he didn't care about it? Were you at fault for not communicating it to him openly?

Communication-related issues are again as common as trust issues in relationships. When partners are unable to open up and be expressive about their needs and wants with one another, they often feel misunderstood and neglected.

Was infidelity the cause for the breakup? Did you find inappropriate text messages and DMs on his phone to other girls? Did you notice him flirting with the cashier in the queue in a supermarket? Did his eyes follow every girl no matter what she wore? Did he reach out to his ex when you were gone for a trip to your parents even though you specifically told him not to?

Unfaithfulness has no excuse. It destroys the foundation of what you two built together. When symptoms of infidelity surface, trust goes out the window. Even when he isn't cheating, in your mind, he is. It is hard to forgive someone that doesn't respect the very basics of being in a relationship with someone.

Was he constantly lying to you? Did he make up excuses for every shortcoming? Did he have his way of manipulating the truth and making you the bad guy in every situation? Did he break your trust with his lies all the time? Did he further blame you for making him want to lie whenever he got caught?

Lying partners are never to be trusted. They can mold the truth however they like. A liar once is always a liar. It's because they have to keep making up stories to keep their lies relevant and believable. Liars don't realize the consequences their telltales have on the purity of the relationship.

Did you or your partner have unrealistic standards for each other? Did you two always fall short on your promises or expect too highly from each other? Did you two mess up all the time? Were you two never content with how you were as an individual and anticipated more from the other?

Having unrealistic standards for each other can also make things messy. Arguments can break out and disputes may arise. If you or he didn't know how to handle slip-ups and admit when they happened, it was only fair that you two parted ways. You weren't meant to be together.

These are some common reasons among many others why couples separate. What was the reason for your breakup? Can you take a minute and think about what went wrong? Can you also ponder over the root causes of what led to it? For example, if you parted ways because your partner didn't trust you, what made them suspect you? Was it how they were brought up? Was it how their friends treated their girlfriends? Why were they possessive of you? Were they the same with other people in their lives or just you?

Investing in the root causes that might have landed in an argument and later a separation is a good place to start. It also gives you something to self-reflect on. When you understand why something didn't go as planned, you can heal faster. You can also learn about your expectations from a potential partner in the future. More importantly, you can learn a lot about the kind of person you are in a relationship with, your demands and needs, and how to express them the next time.

SELF-REFLECT 101: THINGS TO REMEMBER

HOPE FEELS LIKE THE most valuable thing after a breakup. Every singleton holds onto it, as it is the only light in the darkness. With the hope of a better future comes an opportunity to sit back and self-reflect. Some much-needed introspection enables us to explore the significance of our previous relationship and how it changed us.

Asking ourselves important questions, such as what we could have done differently, allows for more control and clarity in upcoming relationships. It also empowers you to become more aware of your needs and mistakes. Your former romantic partner must have done some awful things, but how about you see it from his perspective? How about you put yourself in his shoes and see if you would have done things the same way or not. See your ex as someone who wasn't just a love interest but someone who came into your life for a reason. If he approached you initially, you reciprocated too. What was it that drew you to him? What made you change your perspective later on?

When you get down to self-reflecting, which you will do in a minute, I want you to keep things constructive. I don't want you going down the rabbit hole and feeling hurt all over again. I want you to think logically and clearly without letting your emotions overwhelm your thoughts. Keep in mind that if your partner abused you in the relationship in any form, he did it based on how he felt about himself.

The goal of self-reflection is to regain your self-esteem. Reflecting on your goals will make you aware of the kind of person you are or aspire to be in a relationship with. If negative thoughts do arise, acknowledge them and dismiss them.

As for the set of questions to start the process of introspection, here are a few suggestions:

Who was I at the beginning of the relationship versus the end?: What positive habits and qualities did he inspire you to adopt? How much did you grow as an individual while with him? If you feel that you only became madder, always ready to argue, or short-tempered, it is a sign that he didn't leave a good impression on you. Conversely, if you became compassionate, loving, and selfless while with him, it means that he left a positive imprint.

What did he teach you about relationships?: Relationship management in itself is a great skill to have. If your former partner helped you discover your love language, made you happier, and navigated ways in which serious relationships should be handled, it means that he was a good company to have. Our partners, current and ex both, teach us a lot about relationship management. They bring their own challenges, insecurities, and burdens. How we handle them together as a couple makes us resilient, expressive, and understanding. Was it something that he taught you about relationships too?

Are there some things you would have done differently?: The idea is to not dwell on your mistakes or blame yourself for the breakup but to identify and acknowledge the things you wished you had done differently. Maybe you could have been clearer and determined about your needs or maybe you could have set healthy boundaries from the start. Think of three things you can name at the moment. Then, use that knowledge to have more meaningful relationships in the future.

What three things about your ex did you admire the most?: Was he someone that pushed you to be better? Did he show support and confidence in your skills and talents? Did he boast of your qualities in front of his friends all the time? Did he teach you to be more resilient and independent in life? Recall the top three things that made him lovable. These are the things you appreciate and want in a partner.

If I could go back in time, would I change something about my ex or the relationship?: You must understand the role you played in the breakup. Relieving yourself of all accountability isn't right. No one is perfect and it takes two to tango. Think about the times you could have handled things differently. Think about the things you wished you had or hadn't said. By scrutinizing things this way, you can work on yourself and improve. Be accepting and mindful. There shouldn't be any shame in accepting your mistakes and standing up to them.

Are there any positives you can take from this experience?: The positives don't necessarily have to be qualities of your ex; it could be about learning something new about yourself, the kind of relationships you want to build, and what qualities you hope to find in a new partner whenever you feel ready. Even the most challenging relationships have some lessons to learn from.

What are the absolute no-no (non-negotiable) traits in a partner?: Finally, think about the things you will not want to compromise on the next time. What actions of your ex hurt you the most? What qualities of his did you absolutely despise? What are deal breakers for you in a relationship? Make a list of what qualities you wish to see in a partner. This will lead to greater relationship success in the future.

PART II

WATCHING OUT FOR TRAPS

AFTER NINA HAD SOME time to self-reflect, she found someone new in her life. It was someone her friends wanted to set her up with. They showed her his Facebook and Instagram profiles. He was attractive and handsome. She felt an instant pull toward him. With Jake, she had never felt this gush of butterflies in her stomach.

This was all so new for her. All she knew was this: she wanted to know Mark more. There was something about him that intrigued her. He wasn't her type. He was nothing like the men she had dated or been around. He was nothing like Jake. Yet, she felt like there was something unusual happening.

Upon further insistence from her friends, she went on a date with him. She was the first to arrive at the designated spot. He came five minutes later. As their eyes met, sparks ignited.

"Hi, I am Mark."

"Nina."

"Hey, Nina. Sorry, you had to wait on me."

"That's all right. Let's go in before it gets colder."

As they entered, he asked her for her coat.

"Sure. Thank you."

What was happening? Why was there so much sexual tension between them?

ROUND, ROUND, REBOUND

LIKE NINA, MANY OF you might have been there. You emerge from a broken relationship and within a few days or weeks into your singledom, stumble upon your soul mate. You think to yourself, geez, what are the chances?

So what if he works as an elevator repairman and you meet him outside a bar in an alley when you are hardly sober? So what if he calls you sexy the first time he addresses you and asks for your number? You just connect on a whole different level. Plus, he happens to be good in bed.

But what's with all the awkwardness and silence when you talk about him with your friends? Why do they all try to change the topic as soon as they get the chance? Do you want to tell them so much about how wonderfully the relationship is going and how happy you are? Clearly, they are jealous that you have found someone this amazing. Why can't they accept that you are in love?

It's probably because they know it's not love. You are an emotional wreck, and he just happens to be your rebound.

Rebound relationships are quick and intense. They pop up right after a breakup. They move fast and mostly come with a sense of familiarity reserved for long-term relationships. Unlike traditional dating, the partners take less time in getting intimate and don't feel that customary hesitation.

Although you have just gotten out of a relationship, you don't delay things. You may know little about this man but willingly spend every night with him. You may even start creating future plans with him. Suddenly, you feel ready to move in together, go on trips, get married, and have babies. Unfortunately, as quickly as they move forward, such relationships don't last long.

It's because you haven't done your homework or taken the time to heal properly. You haven't grieved your breakup and given yourself any time to feel ready to date again. Instead, you go for a shortcut and try to erase your ex from your memories altogether by putting in a new picture inside your head. But this can't work, can it? The emotional pain remains there, unprocessed or tended to.

As we discussed in Chapter 1, heartbreak is no different than physical pain. Say you have a migraine or have twisted your ankle. Although you must rest, sleep for a while, or put some ice on your ankle, the first thing you reach out for is NSAIDs. You want to eliminate the pain by taking a shorter route. It does provide temporary relief, but the pain comes back when the effects wear off.

A rebound may be fun and exciting for some time but as reality starts to hit, you begin to notice faults in the relationship. You realize the blunder you have made. You have made the same mistake of falling for the wrong guy yet again because you were too lazy to know what you wanted from a partner or a new relationship. You need to be clear on your demands and expectations so that you don't make the same mistakes you made previously and have your heart broken.

Is This a Rebound or am I in Love?

Unfortunately, real love happens in movies only. In this age and time, love at first sight happens for a few seconds only. You instantly find yourself scrolling through their socials, given that you know them by name. For some, the attraction instantly dies when they see how their timeline is all about how LGBTQ+ is an abomination. For others, the feelings only grow stronger. But how can it be true love when you have just broken up with a partner whom you thought you loved?

It's easy to confuse real love with reel love, aka a rebound, because the brain is still processing through the grief. It is still trying to make sense of what happened and why. A new partner in this equation is just a means to stay distracted so the mind reshifts its focus from the more-complex but important task toward the less-important and easy one.

How about we differentiate a rebound from true love? Here are some telltale signs of a rebound that you, like Nina, are trying not to see.

You have no idea why your previous relationship ended: This is a classic sign where you find it easy to put all the blame on yourself and move on. This shows that not much time has been devoted to some reflection and awareness. Your new partner doesn't need to know the whole story about what happened, but you must be able to tell them why it didn't work. You must at least take some ownership and not completely be oblivious of the responsibility. If you can't do that, it means you haven't fully processed or recovered from it yet.

You don't know a lot about each other but feel like you are in an established relationship: While some like to keep things casual, others want to dive straight into seriousness. After a few weeks of dating, they have established routines, know what they want from their partner, and have future expectations associated with their partner. Does this seem like something you would do or are currently doing? If yes, it means that it is a rebound relationship because you haven't come to terms with the loss of your former relationship. You are trying to stick to habits and routines you had with your ex and with just a new face.

Your partner thinks you haven't gotten over your failed romance: Sometimes, by hooking up with other partners, we tell ourselves that we have moved on. We feel elated at how easy it was and how falsely everyone claimed it would be difficult. But does your partner think the same as well? If he keeps telling you frequently that you still seem to have feelings for your ex, there might be some truth to it. You may not know it but your heart may be covering up hurt feelings, pushing them into a dark corner. This is no way to deal with a breakup. You need to let them out and take some time to heal. Otherwise, any relationship you have will be a rebound.

You talk about your ex frequently: Does his name or actions pop up in random conversations with your current partner? You might have stayed friends with him but this still doesn't justify bringing up his name during conversations. Your new lover may not mind discussing your ex, but if you were in their place, wouldn't it have bothered you in the least? Would it not have made you doubt their intentions about this relationship? If you were in their place, would you have been okay with it?

If you find yourself talking about your ex often, there is a chance you are still in love with him and haven't moved on. This new relationship can't be real love, right?

You compare your ex with your new partner: Do you find yourself comparing your ex's actions with your current partner? Do you keep telling them how good they are and how bad your ex was? Or the other way around? This hints that you are still not over your previous romance. If you constantly compare your current partner with your ex, you will never have the time to notice their good and unique qualities. It will always be a competition about who's best and who isn't. Your new lover will have to keep proving their worth, which isn't fair to them.

You don't open up with your new lover: Is your relationship more physical than emotional? How compatible are you two? What would you say you love the most about your new partner? Do you avoid talking about your ex with your current partner? New relationships should give couples a chance to explore and know about themselves. If this new person is important to you, it is only fair that you learn about them as much as you can. However, if they are the only ones opening up and sharing about their lives while you try to avoid every chance you get to talk about yourself, it is a sign that you aren't mentally and emotionally ready to move on. This is nothing but a simple and pleasurable distraction. If your lover thinks that you seem unsure, put on a fake smile, and don't seem interested in meaningful conversations, then you need to let them go. It isn't fair to them to overshare with someone who doesn't take an interest. If you can't be your authentic self and have been holding back, there is no point in staying in it. Oh, and it's definitely not love.

You want to go exclusive right away: When people start dating, they set a timeline to when to disclose their relationship to friends and family. They don't go online right away and change their relationship status to "in a relationship" overnight. However, if you insist on making things official, if you feel the urgency to tell the whole world about your newfound lover, something seems fishy. It's either that you want your ex to know that you have moved on or everyone else that you have magically healed from your previous relationship and how happy you are. Sure, it makes sense that you want to shout your love from the rooftops, but just after a week of dating? Is your partner on the same terms too? Are they sure you should be doing this? Are you sure you know the guy in and out? Is he the right one for you? There are tons of things you need to think about before going exclusive.

You love being intimate with him: Intimacy feels good. It is a fact. When you are in someone's arms in the most intimate manner, the world feels beautiful. You feel cared for, loved, and valued. It puts you in a good mood, especially when you initiate it. Is it all about sex with your new partner? Can you not keep your hands to yourself? Do you feel you are more physically attracted to him than on an emotional level? Are you using sex as a means to stay distracted? If this is the case, then it is definitely not real love but just a rebound relationship. You crave that closeness. It doesn't matter who provides it. You miss the feeling of being loved, which tells that you still haven't gotten over your past relationship.

You give him mixed signals: Does it often look confused as to what you are demanding? Do you keep changing your likes and dislikes? Do you fake your interests just to get in the good books of this new man in your life? One minute you feel immensely attracted to him. You want to have his babies, go vacation in a cabin, and just have him by your side. And the next minute, you want him to get as far as he could from you. You brush off his initiations, cut his calls, and don't want to meet. This is where you confuse him by giving him mixed signals. If this is the case, you are still very much in pain from your failed relationship. You don't know what you are looking for. You don't know what your expectations are from this new relationship or you simply don't care.

DO REBOUND RELATIONSHIPS EVER WORK?

THERE IS SOME NEGATIVITY associated with the word "rebound." Every time you hear it, it leaves a bad taste in your mouth. Not to lie, it does have a bad reputation attached to it because nearly all rebound relationships end on a bad note. One partner feels used while the other is still trying to heal from a past relationship. It turns things sour for everyone including the family and friends of both partners.

But for some people, just a fraction, rebounds help them grow and emotionally stabilize. For example, if your ex was a classic manipulator and got his way with everything, your self-esteem must have taken a hit. If your partner treats you like a lady, asks for your opinion about everything, and wants to know how you would like to take things forward, it can be a pleasant change. You can restore your lost confidence in yourself when your new partner repeatedly tells you how lucky he is to have you. Even if it doesn't last long with him, it will certainly make you feel better about yourself—something you missed greatly in your last relationship.

Another reason it can be a good thing for some people is that it can help them reconnect with their sexual selves. Couples who have been in a relationship for years often have less sex than those who have just started dating. Sex no longer feels appealing. Therefore, when a new partner enters your life, it can be new and pleasurable. You may reignite your sense of self, know what it's like to be wanted, and enjoy it as much as you can. For those who had been in a more-or-less sexless communion, this can feel pretty good.

However, in most cases, rebound relationships fail and are unhealthy. It's because they aren't built on a steady foundation. Both partners aren't fully ready to take the next step, as one may be too edgy or vulnerable. They enter the relationship in response to their feelings about their breakup. They want to stay distracted. This new person is just a decoy to keep their mind off of the hurtful feelings. Other reasons include the following.

No time for introspection: Every relationship, good or bad, teaches us new things. As both partners are responsible for keeping it alive and instrumental, when it fails, both need some time to recover and figure out what happened. Now enter a new partner in this equation and you have everything confused. You never have the chance to self-reflect and identify what went wrong. When you don't know why it failed, you can't expect to have a healthy relationship right off the bat. You must know how to handle things and situations better for future perspectives. A rebound relationship doesn't allow you the time to do that. As a result, you might end up making the same mistakes you did in your previous romance.

You aren't who you were: There are too many emotions involved. Going right into a new relationship means you haven't had enough time to heal or go through the different stages of grief and mourning. This means you have several unaddressed emotions like anger and hurt. With a new partner, you might try to suppress those and not be yourself. You might even fake being a completely different person because you find your previous self unattractive and emotionally unstable. But for how long do you expect to keep up with this act? Sooner or later, you will have to change and be who you are.

There is too much baggage: Speaking of unaddressed emotions, there is also a good amount of baggage that you have to free yourself from. If you don't do that, you carry it with you in your next relationship. A rebound, in this case, isn't ideal as you need to clear and get rid of the emotional baggage. You may feel fine today but you won't tomorrow when all of it becomes too hard to carry around. At some point, you will break down. Let that time never come by allowing yourself to heal first and not getting into anything hastily.

You are fragile and hurt: There is no denying that after a breakup, you are hurt and in pain. Thoughts about your ex never leave your mind. You are not in your best state of mind. You may end up lowering your standards with a new man. This will only lead to more hurt in the future, so steer clear of any such relationship.

Rebounds make you appear needy: When you start dating just about anybody, it comes off as being needy. You seek validation from a partner and others around you. Being needy is not healthy because you do anything in your power to keep your new partner happy. You end up doing things you wouldn't otherwise. You might even become too clingy or insecure which can turn off your new partner.

It isn't fair to him: I cannot stress this enough. If you were someone's rebound, how would that make you feel? Would you not feel taken advantage of? What if you develop strong feelings for that person while he just considers you a pawn to get back with his ex? Would you not feel cheated when you are on the receiving end? It is unfair that you use someone to feel good about yourself. It is unfair to use someone to get over your ex. Just hold your horses until you are ready to be in a new relationship again.

It will add more confusion: If you haven't had the time to self-reflect, there must be many things that still confuse you about your previous relationship. Why it ended, what the reason was, what you could have done more, etc., are all thoughts running through your head. Now add to that a new partnership with different expectations and needs. Doesn't sound very pleasant, does it? If you think that being with someone else will lead to clarity, then you are wrong. They can't help you unless you give yourself a chance to help yourself.

It's immature: If you are into a new relationship because you want to make your ex jealous, it's petty and immature. This is no way to salvage a broken relationship. There is no point in putting someone else on the pedestal for that. Think about how your actions will hurt the other person.

Think about the impact it will have on you when they break up with you. A rebound is a silly and immature way of handling a breakup.

JEALOUSY MADE ME DO IT

JEALOUSY OFTEN MAKES WOMEN do crazy things. Oh, my ex posted a picture with a work colleague having drinks... I should do the same. But let me just get a bit closer and look a bit happier than him. Oh, he started seeing someone already, let me hook up with one of my close friends to make him jealous. Oh, he is posting about how peaceful his life is, let me put up a status of how blessed I am to be this independent and free.

The race is never-ending. It's a competition without winners. If one does something, the other wants to do the same, only an upgraded version of it.

I know it because I have been in the same boat. Not once but twice. It happened randomly one day when I unblocked my ex for five minutes on Facebook and found out that he was on a trip with his buddies. It had nothing to do with me. He had the habit of planning such trips with his pals. Yet, this time, it felt like he was boasting about it. He wanted me to see how much fun he was having. He wanted to show people that he was single and happy. He wanted to tell the world how bad, manipulative, and dominating I was as a partner.

He wasn't. But it made sense to me that he would do something like this. So, in retaliation, I took a day off from my office and went to the beach. I put on my sexiest bikini and posted a video about how sexy the lifeguard was. It was petty I know, but, then, I just wanted to get back at him. I wanted him to feel hurt that I was looking at and admiring other men. I wanted him to feel sorry for having dumped me by looking sexy. I wanted him to regret being mean to me, cheating on me, and missing out on all the fun we had together.

He didn't.

The point I am trying to make here is that jealousy has never done anyone ever good. You remain stuck in a fantasy that your man would come running back to you if he thought you didn't miss him. He would come begging for your love and loyalty and tell you how big a mistake he made.

Two weeks down the line, I saw him at the movie theatre with the woman he had cheated on me with. He didn't see me. He didn't have to pretend then. But it looked like he was having the best time of his life.

It hurt bad. I had to come back home after the interval because I couldn't take it. I was mad jealous and hurt. Right after, I went for a rebound relationship, searching for the same happiness he had in his eyes. But I couldn't keep up with it. I kept wanting to be someone I wasn't, just to show off to the world that I had moved on, that I wasn't thinking about my ex, that I was happiest with my new partner.

But I wasn't. No amount of crying helped. No amount of screaming and cursing bad words at him helped. What helped was some reasoning with myself. Why was I doing this? Why was I trying to go after a man that didn't care for me? Why did I want him back when I knew he would never change and that vicious cycle of abuse would go on and on again?

Jealousy, my love, is a natural emotion. We all experience it. We envy someone driving a nicer car than ours, we secretly envy our friends for living in a bigger house with a pool, we envy our coworker who got a big raise after just being hired three months ago... the list goes on and on. Jealousy makes us compare ourselves to others. We forget how blessed we are or appreciate what we have. I know it's a crappy emotion but it is what it is. You can't deny that it does make us want to do better and push harder. It is what keeps us on our toes to be our best selves and give our hundred percent.

However, something is strange about the jealousy that arises when we have recently broken up. It's weird because you don't want to be with that person again, yet you don't want anyone claiming him either.

I felt jealous because I assumed my ex was doing better than I was. It was harder to process that he seemed fine while I am an emotional mess. He beat me at every turn. His work life felt more fulfilling; he seemed to have the best co-workers who loved hanging out. His female friends looked hotter than I ever was; he had bought an amazing place with a great view of the whole city. I, on the other hand, was living in the same apartment near the subway station, always busy and noisy. My coworkers had no time to hang out, let alone party on a weekend. There was nothing I could brag about that would compete with what he had. It took me some weeks of therapy and a lot of contemplation to question, why did I care?

I want to save you from the trouble of going to a therapist unless you have to. But before we do that, let's know a bit more about why you feel jealous in the first place? Ask yourself the following questions:

Are you still in love with him or do you care about him?

Jealousy has many layers to it. Are you used to old patterns and behaviors? Have you not fully recovered? Are you thinking about reconciliation?

Are you confusing another emotion for love or are you still attached?

Sometimes, it is difficult to get to the bottom of things and decipher what emotions you feel. You may confuse attachment with love, which is most common among grieving partners. Attachment with your ex reveals that you still haven't moved on. You feel jealous because you think you don't need him anymore, but you do. You think he loved you and still does, but when he doesn't show any signs of love or regret for having lost you, that's when things take a dark turn. You feel surprised at how easy it is for them to move on, leaving you hanging like this.

Are you living your life through your old relationship's lens?

Not many people move on when they should after a breakup. They still remain attached to their exes and want their exes to have the same reaction. If you are jealous and not over your ex yet, you continue to picture your life with him. You still want the same routines and activities. Suddenly, all the pain he caused becomes smaller than his absence. You want him back, even when it means being abused emotionally and cheated on. That's a classic sign that you are jealous of your ex.

Is your ego making you jealous?

Jealousy can often be confused with ego. Your ego comes in the way. It makes you feel jealous. You are reluctant to face yourself in the mirror or take responsibility for the breakup. You have a hard time acknowledging your shortcomings. Therefore, as a defense mechanism, you use jealousy to point fingers at your ex instead of being mature and responsible about it.

SETTING YOURSELF FREE

STAYING JEALOUS WILL NOT only ruin any future relationships you will have but also take away your mental peace. Your jealousy will lead you to stalk your ex on social media all the time, tracking where he goes, who he is with, following after him, and other crazy things that you shouldn't be doing. It's natural to feel hurt but don't let that hurt make you a stalker. You are made for far better things than to camp out at your ex's house and know about all his whereabouts.

This is one reason why blocking your ex from all socials should be the first step. Not having to see them frequently will help you recover faster. If you keep seeing him moving on with his life without you, you will keep sobbing over it. You will want him back in your life, purely because you don't know how to free yourself of this negative and self-harming emotion—jealousy.

But don't worry. Don't lose your mind over it. Pull yourself together. I know you can. Remind yourself that tomorrow will be a better day. Tell yourself that it will hurt a little less. Your ex won't fill the void you feel. He can't undo the hurt he gifted you. Having him around won't make your life any better. All this wanting him back or remaining jealous is in your head. You are safe, happy, and at peace. Don't let your emotions drive your actions.

Now that you have broken up, dissecting the nitty-gritty won't do anything. You can't live in the past forever. It's a trap that will prevent you from recovering. It's one thing to appreciate what you had with that person and focus on the positive memories, and another to want them to become your reality again. Take your time to cherish the happy memories but don't get stuck on them.

You are jealous because you don't have what your ex does: peace of mind. You want it too, but you think only he can give it to you. Love, you have to create it for yourself. You have to find what's missing in your life, within you. You have to remedy your negative emotions by focusing on your personal growth.

Look around yourself and appreciate what you have. Focus your time and energy on the people who love you, are there for you, and support you in all ups and downs. These are the people you should worry about, take care of, and spend quality time with. Eventually, your heart will fill with happiness and gratefulness. You will have no room for jealousy then.

Don't try to reach out to your ex thinking you can still be friends. He isn't your friend, and he is an ex for a reason. Friendship and romance are two different types of relationships, and if you decide to continue with the façade of staying friends, you are only going to make matters worse for your heart. I am not saying that all couples who get back together break up again. It's just there is too much history, lack of trust, and insecurity that comes in between. Old arguments keep surfacing up unless you have resolved them once and for all.

If you have mutual friends together, don't ask them for updates about your ex. You should have nothing to do with how they are doing or what they are doing. Avoid all forms of contact. This includes no driving by their house or workplace, hoping to have a glimpse of them.

If you have to attend any events or parties where you are bound to bump into them, have a buffer with you. Don't meet them alone. You will feel more secure that way. You won't have to carry on with the charade of casual conversation as your accomplice can take over and end it in a few minutes.

Finally, have quick-exit excuses planned in advance. Statements like, "Hey, good to see you [name of your ex]. Sorry, I am running a bit late. I have a hair appointment to get to." You might crash into them on the street or at a café you visited, so be mentally prepared for a brief encounter. Offer an explanation that they can believe instead of just rudely brushing them off. Letting your negative emotions show through your facial expressions might give them the idea that you aren't doing well.

PART III

LIFE POST-BREAKUP

AFTER HAVING HER HEART broken and letting go of the rebound, Nina realized that she had to move on and free herself from any remorse and guilt from her former relationship. During those few months, she had given up so much of herself to please her partner. While looking in the mirror, she couldn't recognize herself. Tears rolled down her cheeks as she tried to remember her happy self. She was such a bubbly girl back then. Jake didn't like the way she was carefree with everyone. He wanted her to be frank with him. He wanted to keep her all to himself. She stopped meeting her friends for lunch like she used to, made excuses to not go to her parents, and ditched her colleagues every time they went out after the office to a bar for drinks.

After all, she had to cook for Jake because he hated take-out food. On her way to her house, she would stop by the grocery store and get the essentials. She would clean up and get into the kitchen. It wasn't that Jake expected her to cook. She wanted to do it, out of love.

I am sure you must have done similar things for your partner when together. You must have made sure that all his needs were met. Even when you were tired to the bone you would make sure that he had everything he needed. If that included ironing his clothes, prepping lunch meals, or finding matching pairs of socks because he was too careless to see where he dropped them... you did it all.

Now is a chance to redeem yourself, your dreams, and your goals. Now is a chance to reconnect with yourself and discover who you really are, as an individual. Because believe it or not, you are complete without a man. You don't need someone to remind you of how amazing you are. You can do it yourself. You should do it yourself.

In this next section, let's learn to fall in love with ourselves. Let's learn how to be compassionate, kind, and generous. Let's learn how to grow and become resilient. Let's talk about how we can upgrade ourselves for the better and become the best versions of ourselves.

And remember, you will not do all these for a man; you will do it for yourself because that's what queens do. They love themselves so much that others have no choice but to fall in love with them.

I AM MORE THAN WHAT HE THINKS

AFTER A BREAKUP, THE first thing that gets crushed is your self-esteem. Poor self-esteem is like a garden weed. If you pluck when it's small, you have a chance to keep your garden blossoming. If you don't, you have to face the consequences of an unruly mess.

When we talk about self-esteem, we often think about our worth. Although self-worth and self-esteem are different things, many people assume it's synonymous. In reality, self-esteem is an elusive and mythical force. It isn't something tangible. You can't grasp it. You have to work for it. It's a lot like how you have to forgive someone and trust them after they hurt you. We all want it to be a simple process, but it isn't. It unlocks many related things like confidence, self-reliance, and resilience. In romantic involvements, it is what boosts our chances of finding someone alike as we seek them with confidence. With high self-esteem, you don't settle. You create your own value. You accept nothing less than what you deserve.

Since it is this powerful, it makes sense why you should have a lot of it. Every queen does. No one can roll an eye at her or refuse her requests. It isn't just fear that makes others follow her. It is her charisma and self-assurance. She knows she deserves to rule the world.

Right now, I assume retaining that level of confidence feels impossible. You have been hurt. You are vulnerable. Your self-worth has never been this low. You doubt everything. Some days will indeed be harder than the rest. It will be hard to get out of bed, let alone regain lost confidence. But I want to help. I must help.

In this next chapter, I want you to look at the girl in the mirror and smile back. Even if the smile feels fake the first few days or weeks, I want you to still do it. I want you to hold your shoulders high and feel proud of how amazing you are.

AM I WORTHY?

AFTER A BAD BREAKUP where many things were said about you, your character, and the way you handle things, it can be difficult to feel love for yourself. I get it, when your heart breaks, your self-esteem gets butchered. He was supposed to be your forever love. You were going to end up with him, have his babies, and have picnics with them. You wanted to spend cold nights snuggled up under a blanket, drinking hot cocoa. You wanted to go on road trips with him. Your wedding day was supposed to be the happiest day of your life. You had it planned out.

But then, things started to fall apart. It felt like the Cupid decided to part ways. Lies and excuses became the norm. You felt unwanted, unvalued, and unappreciated. Yet, you stayed with him, hoping your unconditional love would change him.

But it didn't and it made you feel like a loser. A loser that deserves rejection. You feel like you had the world and you let it go. You feel dejected. All those words said during a conflict about how he hated you kept running in your mind.

There is no escape, is there?

I know how you feel right now. I have been there too. I looked at myself in the mirror and hated what I saw. I knew I wasn't to be blamed for the breakup and still I would find ways to blame myself. I felt unworthy. Unworthy of anything good in life. Unworthy of being loved, taken care of, and made to feel special.

I felt every other man that looked at me felt the same disgust. They could see who I was. Unworthy.

But I wasn't. It was all in my head. I had made myself believe this lie. My inner critic did me no favors either. Instead, she encouraged the idea and reminded me of the many times I had let someone down. A teacher for not doing well on my essay when she had high hopes for me, my parents who were sure that I would choose a college near home, my friends who felt I was making excuses to not meet them when in reality, I was just trying to sort my life together.

After the breakup, such thoughts only multiplied. Their intensity only aggravated. I knew I had to do something quickly or else I would lose all confidence in myself. It took me months to appreciate myself again. Even more to be kind and generous to myself. But I am in a good place today. I want you to be there with me!

Repeat after me: I am worthy of being loved, cherished, and celebrated. I am an exclusive kind. I don't need others to determine my worth. I make my own rules. Only I decide who I want to be with, when, and how. I set my boundaries myself. No one can bring me or my self-worth down. I will never give anyone the power to do so.

Repeat these statements to yourself the next time you look at yourself in the mirror. Regain that lost sense of confidence, refuel your energy, and rebuild. It won't happen overnight but with consistent appreciation and gratitude, you will notice significant changes in how you see yourself.

Appreciate your physique and soul too. You are a beautiful specimen in and out. With time, you will feel less guilty about the breakup and realize your true worth. And might I remind you what that is? You are a *queen*!

SELF-AFFIRMATION: FIRST STEP TO SELF-CARE

SELF-CARE IS AN ESSENTIAL part of rebuilding self-esteem. The thoughts you have influence your actions and behaviors. I am a big supporter of manifestation and the Law of Attraction. I believe that if you manifest good things, the universe brings them closer to you. You attract what you feel. If you constantly doubt yourself, your relationship-management skills, and your ability to keep a man, those doubts will further mess with your mind and actions. Your doubts will be confirmed. Your fears will come alive. You will lose self-confidence. You will feel stuck.

When you develop a particular mindset, you attract what you wish for. If you want more confidence, clarity, and mental peace, then that's what you will get. Just send out a signal into the universe, and I promise it will respond back. If you have thoughts about how you aren't enough and are unworthy of good opportunities, romantic partners, and love, you will attract the same negativity from the universe too.

This is why positive self-talk is the most important pillar of moving forward after any adversity. Positive self-talk or self-affirmation empowers you to practice positive and constructive self-talk. It allows you to reframe your negative thoughts and emotions and feel better. Through self-affirmation, you choose to see things from a positive viewpoint and try to find the good in every experience you have. You focus on the good things you did and be proud of them. This helps you foster self-worth.

So how do you start with the process? Is it as easy as standing in front of the mirror and gloating about how amazing you are? Yes and no.

Yes, if you feel the words you speak about yourself come from deep within, you can start with something as simple as that.

No, because you might stumble upon what to say, when to say it, and how to say it.

Here's what you can do!

Start with creating a list of the things you did in the relationship. What things made you most proud? Were you someone with severe relationship anxiety but overcame it? Did you fear you would never get along with his family but bonded with them easily? Did you overcome your insecurities about your partner and give them the space they needed to be themselves? Did you grow as a person in the last few months or years when you were with your partner?

Recall the times you felt valued and valid. What things were you most proud of? Keep that list with you and look at it often. Add more accomplishments to it, as many as you can remember. Whenever you require some reminder of how amazing you are and what greatness you are capable of, look at that evidence to reframe negative thoughts.

Limit browsing social media excessively especially when you have many mutual friends with your ex. Focus on other more important things. Being on social media, seeing those perfect couples honeymooning in the Middle East, partying, and going to beaches together will make you feel bad about yourself. You may also find pictures and videos of your ex, having a good time without you. You may end up comparing your current situation with him and how happy he looks. If you do feel bad, remember that what you see on social media isn't the whole story. In fact, many times, behind those picture-perfect moments are arguments happening between couples for not taking the perfect shot.

Create a mantra, more like a chant that you repeat to yourself often. Say it out loud whenever you feel anxious, disheartened, or sad. Mantras that boost self-esteem have a calming effect on the mind. It gives you something positive to focus on. They can be your safe haven you come back to whenever you lose your trail of thoughts and feel negativity taking over. I will leave out some mantras for you to get started. However, I personally prefer DIY-ing your own as your situation might be different than mine or others.

Be gracious and thankful for all that your relationship taught you. Think of it as a good thing that happened. Had you stayed with a cheater and remained oblivious, you would never have found true happiness and loyalty. Had you let your feelings run down and be dominated, you would have lived a life full of regrets. Had you tolerated all the anger and possessiveness, you would not have lived freely or wholly. It is a good thing that your relationship ended. Be thankful for that. Now you can focus on yourself, your needs and passions more clearly and find someone much more deserving of you, whenever you feel ready. Changing the way you see your former relationship will help you heal faster as well as move on rapidly.

Make time for people you neglected or didn't spend time with when with your former partner. Appreciate their presence and support. These include your parents, siblings, and friends who stood by you during the hard times and continued to shower you with hope and confidence for a better day. These are the people who you must cherish and be thankful for. When you start spending quality time with them, you will feel much happier. Your self-esteem will increase. Your self-confidence will soar.

Mantras to Repeat to Yourself Daily and Often

- I am worthy of good things.

- I deserve love and care.

- I am getting there.

- I am strong and confident.

- I have the power to move on.

Self-Affirming Statements to Incorporate in Your Daily Routine

- Even if it hurts right now, I know I am worthy of love.

- Being single isn't the end of the world.

- My happiness is my top priority.

- When I feel ready, I will open my heart.

- This pain and hurt are temporary.

- I am stronger than most people.

- I release myself from these negative thoughts.

- This experience was essential for my personal growth.

- In time, I will let go.

- I choose to let go of everything that doesn't serve me.

- I deserve respect.

- I matter.

- I have so much to offer.

- I choose to let go of all resentments.

- I forgive my ex.

STOP WITH THE SELF-PITY

AT TIMES, THOUGHTS ABOUT reconciliation cloud the mind. Maybe I can forgive him, maybe I was too harsh on him, perhaps I should have forgiven him when he apologized... Not only do these thoughts take over, but they also leave you feeling like the bad guy. In other cases, you end up feeling like a victim, dejected and unwanted.

When love is at stake, this happens. People get confused. They miss having someone around. But even if they do get back together, without resolving the core issues, it is only a matter of time before history repeats itself. Even if you forgive someone for cheating on you, you live in constant fear of them doing it again. You keep checking his phone, inquire about his whereabouts every time he is a little late, and cross-question to check if they are lying or not. That isn't fair on him either. Imagine if you were in his place. Wouldn't you feel guilty all the time? Wouldn't you feel like a prisoner in the relationship?

But it makes sense because, in relationships, we go crazy with love. We operate from an emotional mindset. So when your heart breaks, it isn't uncommon for you to go through a dark phase where you question your own existence. You do or say things you would never otherwise. Moreover, you feel responsible for the breakup. You hate yourself among other things that prevent healing and recovery. Healing happens when you accept what happened and feel good about yourself. It happens when you free yourself from resentments and guilt. It happens when you feel whole again, confident, and worthy.

Self-pity is a common theme among women. Every time something goes wrong, they take it upon themselves. So what if your boyfriend is in a cross mood? It isn't your fault. It isn't your responsibility to cheer him up. You can but don't take it up as a job.

Self-pity is when you become preoccupied with your own troubles. You have these unsafe thoughts about how your life has no meaning. You go into a deep depression where nothing matters and you want to quit. You feel abandoned, lonely, and hurt. You feel rejected and cut to the core. However, when this happens, you prevent yourself from seeing what's in front of you. You are so immersed in the "what-ifs" and "buts" that you fail to notice how fortunate you are to come out of an unhealthy, unsatisfactory, and all-consuming relationship. You can't see the forest through the trees, you know what I mean? It's hard to see the glass as half full because you are so doused in self-blame and guilt.

Your days begin and end on a gloomy note. You forget to live in the moment or make the best of it. You let valuable time—time to work on your career, reconnect with friends, and fulfill your dreams—go to waste.

One bad thought leads to another and then another, and the cycle continues. You feel withdrawn from others. You believe the world is conspiring against you. Nothing feels good anymore or brings you joy. When you develop a strong sense of "nothing goes my way," you give up. You leave your problems be and accept them as your new reality.

But it doesn't have to be. Self-pity is an energy suck and you don't have any time for it. You don't need to think about harming yourself because it isn't fair to those who love you and wish to see you happy. It is unfair to your parents and friends who stood by you through thick and thin, listened to your woes when you wanted to vent out, and opened their arms to give you a warm hug when that's what you wanted.

Tell me this: do they deserve to see you like this? Do they deserve the unwanted hurt they feel when they look at themselves as a failure? All because a relationship didn't work out? All because a man left you? All because he couldn't stay loyal?

YOU ARE A STRONG WOMAN, REMEMBER?

WOMEN, AHH, WE WILL tie ourselves in knots of shame and regrets over a simple failing. Forgetting your anniversary, putting out food for the birds, forgetting to check in on your parents, or taking the more busy route to pick up the kids from school... find us berating ourselves over the slightest of mistakes.

During one study, three hundred people between the ages of fifteen to fifty were questioned about some common situations that made them feel bad (Etxebarria et al., 2009). The findings revealed that men are more self-centered than women. Their biggest regrets include eating or drinking too much. They are not angered or guilty over forgetting something important, doing something the wrong way, or being rude to someone unnecessarily. Women, on the other hand, are far more concerned about how they treat others. A man will shrug a mistake off but a woman will become angry with herself. She will turn her guilt and shame on herself. Even if she is winning, like making more than her partner, getting a promotion, or going on a trip with friends, she would feel bad about it. Why? Because she is hard-wired to put others first. She has to think about others, take care of them, and then if time allows, worry about her problems. Men are more driven and committed to their own growth and needs. They want someone in charge to take care of them, nurture them, and validate their importance and value. Men feel pride in doing so because they are men after all. Society has given them a free take on doing things however they want to do them.

For women, the rules are a bit twisted. Women are nurturers and more sensitive to others' needs. They must make others feel good. Women worry too much as well. They have the power to find their fault in every other thing. Women overthink too. Unlike guys, they don't know how to just deal with it and let go. They can't move away from things easily. They have the habit of making simple things complicated. They go over basic things over and over again in the head, trying to guilt themselves, aka feeling sorry for how they are.

And believe it or not, at times, self-pity does feel good. It somehow reshapes how we view blame. For example, you might say something like this to a friend, "Life has always been unfair to me." Somewhere along the line, you want their validation to tell you that how you feel is true. You want them to feel sorry for you because it makes your pain more genuine. It draws attention to your problems where you ask others why bad things happen to you, hoping that they would agree with you and admit it as true. After a while, you start to enjoy the attention you receive so you talk about more negative things in your life.

But we all struggle, don't we? Someone might not have gotten their heart broken by a man, but they are facing financial troubles. Someone might be worried about an ailing father or mother and why they should move them to a nursing home. Someone might be concerned about their future careers and whether they did well on the exams or not.

We all have our own problems. Some like to share and some don't. However, the minute you start enjoying the attention for being vulnerable, that's where things go south.

Since you are a strong woman, someone in control of her emotions, situation, and behavior, let's not fall prey to self-pity. Let's not have thoughts about committing suicide, self-harm, or giving up on love entirely. One wrong relationship doesn't declare you unfit. One wrong partner doesn't lessen your worth. You are as strong as you were before. You are the master of your life, the writer of your story, the queen of your realm. No one can stop you in your tracks. If you have chosen to heal and move forward, the only thing that stops you is you. Overcome your fears, insecurities, and self-doubts. Free yourself from the prison of your own thoughts. Hush your inner critic and anyone that doubts your abilities to move forward.

Queens don't give in to their doubts. They change the way people see them with their confidence and surety in their beliefs. They can achieve anything they have their heart set on.

You are your own person, unique in your ways, loveable, and deserving too. You are generous, patient, and trustworthy. Any man will find you desirable. Any man would want to share a future with you. Any man will feel proud to call you their partner.

GETTING PAST THE VICTIM MENTALITY

FEELING SORRY ABOUT NOT being able to keep a man happy or satisfied enough to do your bidding all life isn't uncommon. In fact, this is one of the most expected responses during the initial days post-breakup. You want to grieve, which is essential, but berating yourself for not being your best when clearly you were isn't fair. Grieving doesn't have to make you feel guilty. It should help with the recovery. A continued sense of victimhood will keep you arrested, glued to your past. With that, a chance to forge new meaningful interpersonal relationships will become challenging.

But you must stop feeling sorry for yourself. You must let go of the past. It no longer defines you; it never did.

To prevent criticism, guilt, and shame from taking over, here's what you can do!

Grow forward by letting old patterns and habits go. Sometimes, we get too attached with things and people in our lives. We can't imagine we can live without them. Freeing up your mind and space will foster acceptance. It will make it easier to move on. It will encourage you to be welcoming of whatever life has to offer. By letting go, you will stop feeling sorry for yourself. Your expectations of others and yourself will align too. You will no longer need their validation or approval. No one will hurt you further either.

Admit that the relationship wasn't adding any value to your life, admit that your boyfriend wasn't the best, and admit that your companionship was lifeless and boring... Admit and accept that things weren't always the best. Admit that fights were breaking out too often. Admit that your partner wasn't being honest most of the time. Admit that you saw it coming. You knew it wasn't going to last. For so long, you have kept the truth hidden from yourself. Face it, even if it hurts. Face it that he was at fault entirely. He cheated because he wanted to, not because you had gained a few pounds over the holidays or gotten busy with work. Face it if you started to nag a lot or probed unnecessarily. If you made mistakes along the way, own up to them. Admire the courage for owning up to your part of blunders. At least you aren't like him, hiding away and making excuses.

Finally, practice mindfulness. If too many negative thoughts are to blame, live in the moment. Focus on your breathing. Let the thoughts come and go without crowding your mind. Don't hold onto them. Release them from your system with every new breath. Thoughts of self-pity will also surface as you try mindfulness but remember to not dwell on them. Let them pass. With mindfulness, you will achieve more clarity. You will become more curious and open. You will regain lost confidence as you work on your self-esteem. Over time, this practice will empower you to focus on the things that help you grow.

"I" COMES BEFORE "YOU"

FOR AS LONG AS I can remember, thinking about myself was labeled as "being selfish." Growing up in a moderately conservative family, I was told to share everything with my brother. But he wasn't taught the same. If he put his hand on something, that was his. I, on the other hand, had to ask before taking it. Parents masked it by being caring and considerate. But I didn't feel any empathy. How could I when I was told to give away the things I loved the most when I wanted them? Be it sharing my toys, Christmas presents, or awards and medals I got from school, my brother could call them his own without asking me.

That conditioning got registered in my system and I started to see it as acceptable behavior. So what if it was killing me from inside? At least, it made everyone else happy. So what if I hated sharing my things—I must because it would be rude not to. So what if I didn't like being mocked, harassed, and cat-called on the streets—that's what young men do.

Stay quiet, put on a smile, and give.

That's what we have been told. Unfortunately, when I entered my first relationship, I didn't know how to handle my emotions, feelings, or partner. I didn't know to set clear boundaries, say no when I felt uncomfortable, or give someone a piece of my mind when they tried to ridicule me. I had to play dumb, be pretty, and laugh even at jokes that made me want to vomit.

It didn't last. The guy lost interest in me after a while because, according to him, I was too conservative. I wasn't open to new things and, thus, not worth his time.

My second relationship was a bit more formal and mature. I had just gotten out of college and started a part-time job. He was doing the same. We interned at a publishing firm together. For once, it felt good to have someone that shared the same interests and hobbies. We had so much to talk about. Be it about books, comics, or the latest movies, it was a never-ending conversation until one day, I randomly checked his phone and found messages from multiple other girls. He had been chatting with them on and off throughout our relationship. Then, it dawned on me that all the late nights where he was supposedly "working on his CV" or "submitting an article for a newspaper" were all lies. He had been two-timing me. But because I was so much in love, always being considerate and understanding of his needs and space, it never occurred to me that he was doing all of it behind my back. I had invested so much in that relationship. I thought he was the one. He clearly didn't share the same ideas.

After spending some time alone with my thoughts, and reflecting on both failed relationships, I realized that I had the habit of giving too much. I got too attached too soon. I had forgotten to put myself first. I had given up on my dreams and aspirations because I felt like I had to. Making home-cooked meals, buying groceries, helping him with his essays, and refining his drafts, all under the disguise of love, was a waste of time. Had I shown the same dedication to my career then, I would have ended up in a much better place sooner.

Putting yourself first should be your first priority. It may feel like the hardest thing but who else have you got besides you? It's ironic how we only realize how good a company our being is when we are left all alone. After a breakup, it's like meeting yourself for the first time. You change so much in the way you look, dress, and feel. It's because you had been dressing up in the kind of styles he liked, eating the food he loved eating, and only allowing yourself to feel happy and grateful for having him around.

Time to wake up and realize that in doing so, you only do yourself wrong.

Learn to invest in things that make you happy. Find things that enlighten your mood and make you feel lighter and happier. A big aspect of recovery involves getting to know yourself better. Find out who you are as a person. What's your personality like? Reconnect with yourself when you were a child. What did you want to become when you were young?

Now that you are free from any shackles or commitments, utilize this time to the fullest by working on yourself. Heal while growing. Grow while healing. Make that your motto. A bad breakup shouldn't stop you in your tracks. It should have never stopped you in the first place. Let go of any reminder that entices pain. Let's focus on how to rediscover who we are, what we crave, and who we want to be, starting with recovering your physical self.

START BY EATING RIGHT

START BY FOCUSING ON your physical health. All queens do. They are presented with special meals that tend to their wellness needs. They need to stay alert, be presentable, and be on their best behavior all the time. A good diet helps you do that. How do I know? Well, have you ever seen a queen yawn, burp, or pass gas during a congregation? It isn't considered very feminine, is it?

Binge eating, midnight munching, and devouring ice cream as if it's your last day on the planet are again common with depressed/sad people. Women are no different. I know that tubs of ice cream hit differently when you have it on your period days or when you are emotionally unstable, but this isn't a healthy way to overcome grief. At the end of the day, you will only gain more weight, have pimples crowning your forehead and cheeks, and fat accumulated in all the wrong places.

How do I know it? It is because I have been there. I felt deserving of treating myself to all the best desserts in the world. Be it cake, donuts, or pastries, I had it all. My sugar intake increased a hundred times when I was grieving my second breakup. It just happened so suddenly that a thousand thoughts ran through my mind. I guess having some comfort food distracted me for a while. But on the fourth day, when piles of wrappers surrounded the trash can, I knew what I was doing wouldn't work. It might temporarily distract me, but the distraction wasn't what I needed. I needed to mourn in healthy ways. I needed to deal with my emotions more constructively.

Moreover, the food that I was consuming was all high in sugar. I didn't feel like cooking so every night was a take-out night. Most days, I would binge on a burger or two with extra curly fries and two sodas to dowse it all in. You can imagine the number of burps, gas, and lethargy. My mind felt numb, almost unworkable. I was too tired all the time. Going to work felt like an insurmountable task. Even if I did make it, the whole day would go unproductive. I knew I wanted help and that's when I reached out to seek professional help. What I learned during those valuable sessions was that indulging in food was a sign that I had given up on myself. My grief had taken over. It's all I could think about even though I had my whole life ahead of me. I knew I would meet someone someday in the back of my mind, but my mind wasn't ready to register that. It was enjoying the many sensations food was arousing. Why would it want to stop?

After every session, my therapist gave me some homework to do. Some were basic questionnaires and others were exercises about hobbies and passions I enjoyed. I was also asked to journal my thoughts and emotions throughout. She told me that my body was my responsibility. I had the power to control how I feel. I had the power to decide how I wanted to feel. Nourishing and caring for my body by giving it the right fuel was the only way to go back to feeling healthy, active, and alive.

So I gave it a try. I purged my cabinets and got rid of anything that didn't look healthy. This included biscuits, candies, chocolates, and chips. But by evening, I was craving the same things again. So I looked at alternative options. I noticed triggers and cravings. What was my body really craving? Was it chocolates or just sugar? Was it something greasy or just some comfort food? Was it chips or something to munch on? You get my point, right?

Sometimes, cravings come disguised as other more tempting things. You need to decode the real reason why you want to eat something. What's the reason behind it?

Since it wasn't realistic to start a diet the next day and go on all-greens, I decided to gradually put myself off the foods I loved. How did I do that?

By choosing alternatives.

- If the body needed sugar, I went for a tablespoon of honey, sometimes half a tablespoon of peanut butter, or a cup of Greek yogurt with some fruit.

- If my body craved fatty foods, I got a packet of frozen store-bought raw potato and sweet potato fries. Then, instead of frying them in oil, I baked them. Now I air-fry them.

- If my body craved something comfy like mac-n-cheese, I substituted it with whole-grain pasta for my base. I also reduced the amount of cheese I would previously add. Just enough to remind me of how good this tastes.

Notice the difference? I was giving my body the same things it craved but in the way I wanted to.

Do it and see the difference in terms of how energized you feel throughout the day, ready to be on your toes. You will also feel clearer in the head, focused, more productive, and alert. These are only some of the benefits of eating healthy. This shouldn't just be a post-breakup ritual, but something you should incorporate into your everyday routine.

Add to your diet foods high in serotonin (Dfarhud et al., 2014). It is your happiness hormone. The more you have it in your body, the easier it will be to find things to be happy about. Such foods elevate your mood, boost the brain's function, and improve the quality of sleep. Foods high in serotonin include bananas, eggs, yogurt, turkey, beans, and nuts.

MOVE, MOVE, MOVE...

THE NEXT THING YOU need is to get your heart pumping. Moderate exercise is an important component of any form of recovery. Since your heart has been broken, your dreams shattered, and your hopes about finding true love are at an all-time low, clearing the system of unwanted stress is the way to go. Through exercise, you don't only burn calories. You can also leave unhelpful thoughts and emotions behind you. With every step you take in the direction ahead, imagine leaving behind all painful memories.

Countless research tells us how exercise releases the feel-good hormones in the body, which elevate mood and evoke feelings of happiness. With breakups, a lot of unwarranted stress enters the body. The mind feels occupied with negative thoughts, the body feels heavier with all the pain and guilt you carry, and your soul feels deprived of happiness. This is all because of the increased production of cortisol in the body. It triggers anxiety and panic attacks. You find yourself worried sick, defenseless, and without support. You get stressed over the slightest of issues because the mind is preoccupied with the wrong thoughts. Thoughts about what if something goes wrong, what if I end up all alone, what if no man finds me attractive ever again, etc.?

It is important to nip such thoughts in the bud and one of the most effective ways is through exercise. Start with any form of physical activity that gets you moving. You don't have to leave the house if you don't feel like greeting your neighbors or meeting friends. You can start with a simple workout from YouTube and begin.

It's understandable if all this seems too daunting and difficult. But you have to start somewhere. Maybe not today, but make it tomorrow's goal. If you have a big space in your house, simply walk for 10 minutes. Allow yourself to immerse in the act. Remember throughout that you are doing it for your own good.

You can also mix it up with some tunes of your choice and get moving. Dance routines, yoga, and meditation are also different forms of exercise. They each promise a different set of benefits but the essence remains the same: release of stress-inducing emotions, better sleep at night, and more mental clarity, aka the three things that will help you move on.

JOURNAL AWAY YOUR BROKEN HEART

BREAKUPS ARE PAINFUL. APART from who takes the dog, who moves out, and who keeps the coffee maker, there is a heart that needs mending—actually two. Despite how it ended, I am sure your partner takes away some guilt and anger with him too. But right now, you need to focus on yourself. Put yourself first, remember? Journaling is one of the most recommended and practiced forms of activity to vent out suppressed emotions. It is a therapeutic process where you write down your feelings to release them out of your system. With journaling, you can identify the emotions you feel, what triggers them, their cause, source, and how to cope with them.

When you jot down your emotions on paper, you have a chance to work through difficult emotions. The same emotions you had been running away from suddenly don't feel that scary. It is an effective method to challenge your negative thoughts and come up with healthy ways to deal with them. You can also manage your anxiety levels and stay calm throughout the many phases you go through.

I remember when I began journaling my thoughts; there wasn't much to write at first. For starters, the whole practice felt awkward because although I was used to writing stories and articles, this felt unusual. How can you pen down what you are feeling? Who are you speaking to? Do you begin with "Dear Diary" every day? Despite these thoughts, I started to write and made it a rule to write at least a page every day. After a while, I started to notice a pattern. All day, I would think about what I wanted to write today and it kind of made me excited to get down to it. I focused more on things that were scripting-worthy. If an emotion overpowered another during the day (like sadness over happiness), I made sure to mention it in my journal.

I believed that the best way to journal was to be as raw as possible. Say things like they were. No censorship. I was brutally honest and elaborative about how I felt. I didn't make myself appear smarter, prettier, or better. I made sure to include the stupid mistakes I made in the relationship without any shame because I knew no one was going to read them.

I also made sure to write more on days when I felt bad, unwanted, and depressed. It helped me calm my nerves and restore my usual self. Some dark days became bearable because I felt I had someone to talk to. Don't forget that self-talk is the best talk of the day.

Some days, I had nothing to write about. I felt tempted to skip. However, I didn't. Instead, I used powerful prompts to let all the guilt, anger, and hurt out. For example, you may ask yourself these or similar questions:

- What do you miss/not miss about your relationship the most?

- What behaviors will you never tolerate again in a potential partner?

- If you meet your ex today, what would you like to tell him?

- How did the ordeal help you grow?

These types of prompts will get the juices flowing and bring out those deep, hidden, and often neglected emotions you kept locked in. If you want to fully recover, which I know you do, you will have to deal with them.

You can't let them ruin your life and important moments in life. You can't allow them to hold you back from approaching new love. You won't.

Another great idea is to write about what you want your future to look like. Who would you like to have in your life? Who would you like to let go and distance yourself from? What fun things do you want to take up? What places do you want to visit? What cultures do you want to know more about? What new resolutions do you want to set? All these are some exciting questions that will help you move on faster. If what awaits you is interesting, adventurous, and thrilling, why waste time?

THE RISE OF A QUEEN

HAVING YOUR PHYSICAL NEEDS taken care of, the next thing that pops up in your mind is your emotional and mental well-being. How are you going to take care of your mind and soul? How will you nourish it? How will you heal and move forward?

Your mental and emotional well-being is as important as your physical wellness. What's the point of having good health when your mind remains corrupted with negative thoughts and your soul upset? You may eat well, exercise, and pen down your emotions. If you still feel discontent, worried, and stressed out, what good will it do? Emotional and mental health goes hand in hand with your physical health.

It's like you have filled your car with gas, and now you need someone who knows how to drive. A car filled with fuel is of no use if you don't know how to drive. Similarly, a car without fuel won't get you anywhere either. So the connection between the two is as strong as day and night. One has to come after the other. The night has to surrender to dawn for the day to break.

Emotional well-being isn't something we focus on a lot. Although it is important to know what's going on in your head, and what thoughts drive your actions and behaviors, we rarely take out the time to work on it. We take things as they come without any awareness as to why they are happening, what emotions trigger them, and how to deal with them.

Our mental health affects how we think, feel, and behave. Not investing in its wellness leads us to unwanted, self-inflicted thoughts that further attack our self-esteem and confidence. After a breakup, emotional and mental health takes a toll. The wrong kinds of thoughts cloud the mind. They dissipate energy, take away focus, and leave us feeling vulnerable. We end up questioning our true worth.

Right now, what you need is some encouragement and willpower to work on your mental and spiritual needs. What is it that your mind craves? What is it that your soul desperately searches for?

Some peace, some hope, or perhaps both?

Let's learn how to work on ourselves, from our mental and emotional needs to our appearance and confidence. Let's build a life that makes you happy and blessed. You deserve it.

Doing so is also important for your self-esteem because sooner or later, you are going to meet someone special again. You want them to love you for who you are – strong and confident, not weak or insecure. In any relationships you develop, you have to play an equal role. Be it a new friend you make in your neighborhood, or a new colleague you helped get settled in, you will have to play an equal part in sharing that bond. Be it a potential partner your friends set you up on a date with or someone you meet at a bar, your contribution and interest are as important as theirs.

Besides, after this failed relationship, you don't want to end up making the same mistakes again. And by mistakes, I mean not knowing what type of attachment style you have, what you look for in a partner, and what type of relationship you are looking to have. You also need to know what things you would allow and disallow in a relationship, what character traits you will never compromise on, and what your expectations are from your partner from the get-go.

All these are things you will think about once you have healed and achieved some clarity.

This brings us back to nourishing your mind and soul.

Together, let's promise to live life to the fullest and make the future an amazing place to be in. These come highly recommended by relationship coaches and marriage counselors to lessen the pain caused by a breakup, separation, or death.

LIVING YOUR BEST LIFE – YOU OWE IT TO YOU

IF YOU ARE NEWLY single, the idea of moving on in life without your ex might not be your first one. After all, you were sure he was the one. You were confident that one day you would say your vows to him. You imagined having three kids running around the house while you two happily make pancakes in the morning, kissing each other occasionally. Yes, I know the visual will not be a reality any longer. But your ex didn't think about all those things. So why stay drowned in his memories and not move on? All that's left for you is to move on and accept that person isn't going to be a part of your life.

What you can do is make the most of your free time. You are single and available. The world should be your oyster. Don't you want to just go out and party whenever you like? You can go to brunch with your girlfriends any time you want without having to worry about your partner feeling jealous. You don't have to stay in and spend your weekends with him and pick a fight over what to watch on Netflix. Damn woman, you can watch *Legally Blonde*, *Bridget Jones's Diary*, and *Kill Bill* all on the same day!

You can go out to places you stopped going because your ex didn't like the food. You can spend as much time as you want with your sister or parents without having to worry about your partner getting bored. You can get enrolled in those salsa classes you so wanted to get into, but your partner didn't think it was very wise of you.

There is so much that you can do. Correction: must do it now that you are free to do it.

Let's explore some more ideas as such to keep things rolling for you without you missing your ex. No need to waste any more time on him or his stupid arse.

Embrace this newfound independence and make the most of it. Start with a list of things titled Things I Missed Out On. Then, spend time doing those things and feeling whole and happy again.

First, hang out with the people you had been avoiding. An old friend with whom you had a platonic relationship that your partner didn't want you to continue, a girlfriend he said was too full of herself, a cousin he didn't enjoy hanging out with. Go for a brunch all by yourself or with your closest pals and load up on eggs benedicts. Catch up on everything you missed talking about. There is nothing better than this to have your mood drastically improved.

Try going for a solo trip. It could be a one-day or weekend trip. You don't have to cross continents either. Start with the cities next to yours. Worried about going alone? Don't. There are tons of tour companies that take tours in group forms. Surely, you will find someone like-minded. If not, remember that you are your best company. Enjoy this peaceful time, basking in the sun and taking in the beautiful landscapes, buildings, and monuments.

Change your surroundings. If thoughts about your partner never leave your mind, maybe a change of scenery will do. Take a sabbatical from work and go live with someone else for a while. Get out of the house you two built together. If this isn't possible, start going on walks or going grocery shopping. Getting out of the house, even for an hour or two will help clear the mind and make you feel less gloomy.

Make time for your hobbies and passions. Did you give up painting because your partner didn't appreciate the mess it created in the room? Did you enjoy dancing and singing but your partner thought you needed to grow up? Did your partner not approve of your flea-market DIYs because they seemed tacky? Well, now that he is out of the picture, go back to doing all those. Make time to rejoice in the happiness they promise. Enroll in a dancing class, sign up for advanced pottery lessons, or make your trips to flea markets more frequent. He can't stop you now, can he? Then why give up on the things you love?

If you have no passions, it's an ideal time to take up a new hobby. Go on a hike on weekends, learn a new language, volunteer at a pet shelter, organize your closet, repaint your walls, upgrade furniture pieces, make a cooking video, and learn a new workout. Find something new and interesting to improve how you feel. Invest in those hobbies by making time for them in your daily routine. There are literally a thousand things you can do. Just start with whatever feels easy and, as Nike puts it, just do it!

Another great idea, if time allows, is starting a side hustle. Do you have a knack for cooking? Do your friends always ask you for recipes and cooking hacks? Start a YouTube channel or make daily vlogs. If you love dressing up or doing makeup, make an Instagram account where you can showcase your skills. If it takes off, you will get brands to sponsor your videos and earn. Create reels and short videos to gain followers and subscribers and start earning. If you get compliments on your DIY jewelry, create some for friends for free and then ask them to advertise it for you. Soon, you will start getting orders. If you have excellent writing skills, how about writing articles and books? Self-publish on Amazon and become an author. If you can't come up with an idea for a book, narrate your struggles with heartbreak. Building a business, no matter how small, takes effort, dedication, and time. Luckily, you have all three!

Do a mini remodel of your place to make it your own. Remember the time you were at Target and wanted to get those cushions for the couch and your partner said they were too feminine? Guess it is time to get them now that you have the place all by yourself. Remodel and renovate. Go to IKEA and get everything you wanted but didn't take because your partner didn't want to make the place look like something from *The Sisterhood of the Traveling Pants* movie. Redecorate. Don't invest in everything new. Look up yard sales and flea markets near you and spend your weekends for a much cheaper haul. You can also DIY old frames with new pictures and paint your room's wall in a color of your choice. The idea: just don't hold back. Remodeling furniture, changing where they were placed before, and going for some upgrades will make the place feel homely and yours. It won't remind you of them anymore.

Read. I personally believe reading is the best form of therapy there is. Be it a book about different cultures, a leader's biography, memoir, or an erotica novel, there is so much that a book offers. Read about how to live life to the fullest, read about the struggles of people in the past, how they lived, the industrial revolution, how things changed in the last decade, or about a boy who lived on a farm raising horses. Read about anything your heart desires. Take up on some satirical narrations. They are the best kind. If you don't have the time to pick up a book as you juggle between your work and your new independent life, audiobooks and podcasts are just as good. Listen to it during the commute or before going to bed.

Create new goals. Goal-setting gives you something to look forward to. A goal can be short-term or long-term. You can take a 30-day challenge of some sort, start a new diet or workout regime, improve your sleep quality, or make a goal of staying happy. Take up something new such as learning a new language or musical instrument. Create subgoals to ensure you stay on track and progress. Use to-do lists to jot down the steps you need to reach your ultimate goal. For example, if you want to learn to play the violin, the first subgoal would be researching institutes or instructors near your area. Another subgoal can be finding a music store to get your hands on a new violin. This way, by completing your subgoals one by one, you will get closer to your actual goal.

Finally, take some time for much-needed "me" time. Make it a daily ritual to do something that makes you utterly happy and relaxed. For example, on Mondays, you can light up some candles, fill a glass of wine, and take a long bath. On Tuesdays, you can dress up and go on a date with yourself. On weekends, you can book an appointment for a hairstyle change or spa treatment. Pamper yourself the way you would like to be pampered. Do the things others expect their partners to do for them. You are in full control here. You don't need a man for these.

TIME FOR A STYLE UPGRADE

NOW THAT A MORE amazing and wholesome life awaits you, why embrace it with the same old you? It's high time you go for a shop and dress the way you have always wanted to. A lot of times, our partner's likes and dislikes take over our sane judgment. Suddenly, we want to look good for them. We want to dress the way they like, wear perfume they approve of, and wear accessories they are okay with. It might not have been an issue in your relationship but if I talk about mine, my ex hated any bling on me. Even a bracelet as thin as a thread would put him off. He didn't like me wearing shades of red either, saying it made me come off as "asking for it." The same applied to red lips, any bold eyeliner, or blush. He said he loved me the way I was, all natural. Ironically, the many women he had been texting were everything he didn't want me to be like. Having stalked them in my darkest moments, they all seemed to wear provocative clothing, have their hair down, and wear dark red lipstick. Apparently, my ex loved the way they look.

Shocking, isn't it? If I didn't know him well, I would have thought that he had a polar disorder. He was something else with me and a whole new person with others.

Coming back to the point, as I don't want this discussion to become about him, I want you to look at yourself in the mirror and think about all the things you would like to change. Would you like to have your hair dyed a different color, go for a new hairstyle, or have your hair curled or straightened? Looking at your face, what shades of lipsticks had you been dying to try on but didn't? What statement jewelry pieces do you keep away locked in a jewelry box to never be worn again?

It's time you take them out and wear them with confidence. And let's be clear: you don't want to do it to get back at your ex or try to win him back. You do it for yourself, for your own happiness and pride. You must upgrade without losing your value. You need to upgrade to feel good about yourself. Sometimes, even a small change in the way you look can lift your confidence and boost your self-esteem. You may feel like a completely new person altogether.

Let's start with the very basics: clothing. First up, separate any pieces that your ex got you. Get rid of them. Give them to charity if you feel uncomfortable wasting them. If you are left with only a few items, great! It's time for shopping. Don't buy things all at once. Go easy and start with some basics like office-wear shirts, skirts, a cocktail dress, or a sweatshirt for winters. Then, gradually build your wardrobe as seasons change. For summer times, get a few loose floral frocks, cool prints, and comfortable footwear. Similarly, for autumn, get clothes in warmer tones along with a new pair of boots.

Get professional help from a consultant or fashion blogger to find what style suits your face cut, body shape, and skin tone. The more knowledge you have, the better you can style your outfits. You can ask one or more of your friends to accompany you if you still don't know what to wear and carry. Preferably choose someone who dresses well.

Next comes everything else, basically. This is the epitome of self-care. Self-care hasn't done anyone wrong ever so take up the habit of looking after yourself. Look after your skin, hair, and nails. No one likes to have dry heels, cracked nails, and a dull face. If you plan on falling in love again (which you should), then these are some of the things you will have to take care of. There is no lie that we talk to people who dress well and look well. How you look is the first thing anyone notices about you. So here's what I want you to do.

Book one session each for a haircut, nails, and skin. Go for a hairstyle change or dye. Try something new and exciting, given you have grieved fully. If you had long hair all your life, how about a chop, something like an angled bob or pixie. If you always had short hair, how about getting some extensions and a hair dye? Ask your hairstylist what would suit your face and skin tone. Also, inquire about any products you can buy and use at home for more luscious-looking hair.

For your nail appointment, start with a nice mani-pedi. Your hands and feet will thank you. Manicures and pedicures get rid of any dry and dead skin. They give your hands and feet an instant glow after some much-needed exfoliation and massage. Then, work on your nails. Get acrylics or gel nail polish if you are comfortable with them. Even a simple French manicure will do.

Finally, get your skin checked by a dermatologist. Ask them about good moisturizers, sunscreens, and vitamin C serums. Start a day and night skincare regimen to have glowing, glass-like skin that looks fresh and hydrated. Every month or bi-weekly, sign yourself up for a spa treatment including facial and massage.

Reinventing yourself should be about recentering your focus on yourself. It should make you feel good, important, and valued. It should evoke feelings of gratitude about how healthy and stylish you look. A reinvention will make you more comfortable stepping into the world again. It will make you feel more confident about yourself. Since confidence is the sexiest thing a woman can wear, this ought to make you feel desirable.

After all, someday you will want to approach someone romantically again. So what if a relationship didn't last forever? Someone is waiting to be with you. There is someone out there who will love you with all their heart, love you for how you are and feel pride in calling himself yours. Let's not discourage them from finding you when you don't look or feel your best.

PART IV

WHAT'S NEXT FOR ME?

AFTER A FEW WEEKS of dating the new man, Nina started to see how misfit they were. There was nothing common between them other than wanting to get physical. There were so many other things that she was just finding out about him. Things that she felt she shouldn't have to deal with, given that they both were mature people. There was no emotional connection between them. The thought of having to carry this relationship forward bothered her.

But she didn't want to break up with him either. Her ego didn't allow her. She felt that if she broke up with him now, everyone would blame her for being a bad partner. They would assume that she was the reason why her last relationship didn't work out. She wanted to keep her grace. She wanted her friends to not talk behind her back about how she had made yet another mistake.

It all seemed too confusing. Mark was becoming unbearable to live with, day by day. He wasn't her type. Their mindsets clashed. Their opinions differed. They couldn't come to agree on a single thing. There were no real feelings. At first, she tried to compromise and let Mark do things his way. But it didn't take her long to realize that she had done the same in her previous relationship. She had given up the power she held.

And then it dawned on her: her new beau didn't suit her because he didn't meet the criteria she had. He wasn't what she was looking for. It was all a mistake just to make her ex feel jealous and come crying back. He was nothing but a pawn for her. She was trying to convince herself that she had moved on, but had she really?

LEVELING UP – HELLO NEW LOVE

AFTER MY BREAKUP, I wondered if there was light at the end of the tunnel or not. Even if it were there, it didn't look bright. I didn't know how soon I should approach new partners, what to look for in them, what expectations to have, and what changes/improvements I needed to make to not end up in a failed relationship again.

It is hard to know what attracts you. What qualities must a man have to make me fall in love with him? Should he be kind and gentle? Should he open the door for me when in the car and pay for my food? Should he be funny and intelligent? Should he be compassionate and loyal? What if he has some of these qualities but not all? Is he still an eligible catch?

When you get out of a long-term relationship, it can be hard to define what's considered normal. Your habits and routines have changed. You have changed as a person. If you haven't had a lot of experience with heartbreak, you might never know what's acceptable and what isn't. This means there is a chance that you end up falling for the wrong kind and regretting it later on.

Let's do some introspection, one last time. Let's see what standards to set for a new relationship whenever you plan to get in one. Knowing what you are seeking from a potential partner, how you want the relationship to move forward, at what pace you want it to go, and what behaviors are totally unacceptable, you can enter a new companionship with a clear mindset and expectations.

But first, are you really ready for a new relationship?

Self-Assessment: Am I Ready for a New Man In My Life?

If you are looking for signs that tell about your readiness to step into a new relationship, here are ten:

1. You no longer hold onto painful memories. You can deal with the negative emotions now with a positive outlook. You can visit places you used to visit with your ex without any unpleasant emotions.

2. You can browse through your socials without having the urge to click on their profile and see how they are doing.

3. You can let go of the gifts and things they left

behind. You are no longer attached to them emotionally.

4. The idea of meeting new people, dressing up, and going on a date excites you.

5. You know what boundaries to set and how to put them forth assertively.

6. You have found healthy coping mechanisms to deal with the breakup. You enjoy spending time on your hobbies and interests.

7. You have complete control over your mood and behaviors. You don't allow negative emotions to take away power from you anymore.

8. You can now clearly see your past relationship for what it was. You know why it failed and who was at fault.

9. You are more aware of the deal breakers for you in a relationship. You know what you will and won't tolerate.

10. You feel whole again.

You might think that your self-assessment exercise ends here, but it doesn't. There's so much more you need to prepare for before you go into another relationship.

Why?

It's because I don't want you making the same mistakes I did. I don't want you making difficult choices because you stepped into a new relationship blindly. Once you commit to a new partner, there is no going back. When you break up, you will be back to square one.

If you have found someone who looks compatible and interested, before you head into a commitment, ask yourself what they have to offer. Are you seeking those qualities? How do they add value to you? Will giving them a chance improve your quality of life for the better? What is it that you feel is missing from your current life?

Looking back at your past relationship, how far do you think you have come?

Are you again falling for someone with the same qualities as your ex? If this is the case, you already know where the relationship will lead to. This means that once again, you will have to compromise on the things you promised yourself you won't compromise on the next time. Is he a bad boy or disrespectful? You should know the difference. Does he have commitment phobia or just like to take things slowly? Again, you need to know that in advance. Does he have difficulty expressing his desires or like to put you first? There is a *huge* difference between the two.

Second, know what values and characteristics are important to you in a partner. You might settle for less, and I can't have you doing that. Know what traits define a real man to you. Then, hold onto those traits and find someone that ticks off all of them on the list.

Third, you must know if you are looking for an "opposites attract" kind of relationship. Meaning, are you looking for qualities you don't have? This might suggest that you need to work on yourself some more first, then go out and seek a partner.

Finally, what concerns you more: whether he is the right person for you or you are the right person for him? The way you think about a potential partner and yourself is what sets the standard. It tells whether you are going to put your needs first or his. If you steer more towards his needs, you lack self-esteem. You are still not there where you should be after all the self-reflection. You are still selling yourself short. If this continues, you will fulfill his needs but have yours remained unfulfilled.

When you have answers to those questions, you may feel ready to enter a new relationship. However, all healthy relationships require being your true self. Having someone to share your life with is truly an amazing feeling but it shouldn't make you want to rush things. Are you comfortable with the idea of replacing your ex with a new man? Are you ready to meet the demands of this new partnership?

Do you feel strongly about yourself and your identity? What kind of trajectory are you hoping for? What voids do you want this relationship to fill? The point I want you to think about is whether you feel attracted to the man or the idea of being in a relationship.

Sometimes, we confuse a need with a desire. If you are in love with the idea of being in love and not necessarily attracted to the man, you may end up pushing him into boxes he doesn't fit in. You may desperately try to force a spark when there is none. You may overlook red flags because, in your mind, you are convinced that this will work.

Do you enjoy his company or do you just enjoy hanging out? Is the attraction purely physical or would you have still dated him if he looked different? Do you miss him when he isn't around or is it that you don't want to be all by yourself?

If you can't decide, start by building an inventory of things that attract you to a man. Build a list of what you seek in a relationship and things you will allow/disallow in an ideal romance. Set your expectations and standards. Don't accept subpar standards and don't compromise on your needs. You already tried doing that and look where it got you.

Creating a list of expectations and standards might seem wrong on many levels. You can either be too easy or harsh with your demands. So how do you know if your demands from a new partner are reasonable or not?

Are My Demands Reasonable?

EXPECTATIONS ARE WHAT MAKE people remain committed. If your relationship or partner has no expectations from you, it means that you can treat them the way you find appropriate. Setting realistic expectations from the get-go is important. If you want a sustainable relationship with someone, it is important you two respect each other, have healthy boundaries, and know appropriate ways to show love and receive it. Without expectations and clear notions about what's acceptable and what isn't, misunderstandings arise. You can't always read your partner's mind, can you? Then how do you expect to know what they seek?

So how do you go about setting expectations with a new partner or relationship? What if you end up asking too much or too little? What if your expectations aren't realistic or achievable? How can you evaluate the success or failure of a relationship when you don't have any scale to measure it? Therefore, together, let's create a list of five qualities or traits that you seek in a man and relationship. For me, these five set the standard and quality of any new (intimate and nonintimate) relationship I develop.

For any relationship to have a solid foundation, it must be built on trust. Trust is what keeps partners from becoming insecure. It is what allows them to be their authentic self, fearlessly. Trusting my partner doesn't mean that I turn a blind eye to whatever he does. It means that I have faith in the fact that he won't hurt me. I have faith that he won't do me wrong. I have faith that he will look after me, love me, and cherish me.

To me, shared affection and appreciation also hold value. I expect my partner to appreciate me for all the work I put in. I want him to appreciate me for all that I do for him, for the things I compromise on just for the sake of his happiness. He should expect the same from me. Similarly, he deserves to be appreciated for all that he does. He deserves appreciation when he goes out of his way to do something for me. It's a valid demand to have from your partner that they never forget how much work it takes to make a relationship work.

Speaking of appreciation, it is also a reasonable demand to expect your partner to be equally devoted. It isn't solely a woman's responsibility to look after the house, clean, cook, and do laundry. You are both in the relationship and therefore, take responsibility for it as equals. I expect him to fill in where I fall short and vice versa. He shouldn't hold all the power in the relationship.

No two people are the same. It means a clash of opinions is a real thing. However, if I am ever made to feel like my advice or opinion remains unheard or is rejected, it will be a major turn-off. Both partners should respect the difference between them and understand that they come from different places, backgrounds, and upbringings. It's okay to have a difference of opinion over things. However, your partner shouldn't dismiss your views just because you are a woman and don't know better.

WHAT ARE DEAL BREAKERS FOR YOU?

WHEN YOU INVEST YOUR time and effort into a relationship, it's hard to move away from it. The familiarity of behaviors and routines doesn't let you. You excuse abusive behavior as normal even though it makes you miserable. You don't want to start all over again. It would mean moving out, finding a new social circle, and disappointing your family and yourself. Going through heartbreak is devastating and you want to avoid feeling that way.

But after giving your partner chance after chance to stop the manipulation, dominance, and abuse and correct themselves, if they continue with it, breaking up is the only solution. Now that you are in a position to better assess the qualities you want in a partner, how about making a list of what isn't acceptable? For future preferences, how about knowing what qualities and traits you will absolutely detest in a new partner, whenever there is one?

This will give you the power to decide what works for you and what doesn't. You can establish healthy boundaries from the start and be clear about your expectations. You can tell your partner how you would like to be treated and hope that they follow through.

For example, I will never settle for a habitual liar. If a man thinks he can get away with dishonesty, then he isn't welcome in my house or my life. He's unreliable. His word is unreliable. If you catch your new man often lying to his boss, friends, or colleagues over trivial things, he is definitely lying to you as well. You can never trust a liar because, with habitual liars, the lies never stop.

He cheated on you. Always remember that you have no obligation to put up with a cheater because you have been with him for a long time. Cheating isn't an isolated event. It doesn't just happen. It isn't normal or a one-time thing. If you want to give him another chance, that's between you two. However, once a cheater, always a cheater.

He expects too much from you. Are you his maid, bank account, and cook? Does he not share household chores with you? Does he leave behind his messes for you to clean up? This isn't normal. He needs to do better. He mustn't shoulder you with all his responsibilities too. Don't do them out of love. Set him straight or tell him to pack his bags.

If he emotionally abuses you, convinces you of things you don't feel comfortable doing, and mostly gets his way with things, he is an emotional abuser. Emotional abusers try to put their partners down, control them, or make them feel less about themselves. They may give ultimatums or shut off emotionally for days if you don't do the things they want you to do. Whether you agree or disagree, to me, it's an abuse of the worst kind because it makes you rethink your stances. Don't let him do that.

Does he give ultimatums without decently discussing things? Do you feel you have little say in the relationship? Does he expect you to dress up for a party with his office colleagues even though you told him multiple times how lonely you felt there? If he still insists, don't let things get too far. He isn't the right man. You shouldn't have to live this way.

Does he refuse to discuss serious stuff? Does he change the subject whenever you talk about marriage or kids? Does he refuse to accept his mistakes when you point them out? Does he become unresponsive when you try to make him understand something? Postponing important discussions doesn't suggest a healthy relationship. It's another deal-breaker.

An Ideal Candidate Awaits

This final chapter is a bonus chapter because I don't want you to rush into another relationship right after your previous one. You need time and understanding of your emotions. You need to acknowledge their existence and learn healthy ways to cope with them.

Then, once you have done all the work, come to terms with your failed relationship and feel ready to give love another chance. Then, by all means, feel free to give this brief but important chapter a read.

It's all about how to attract the right man for yourself, the one who will shower you with love, appreciation, and respect. He will not make you change yourself. He will not make unnecessary demands like giving up on your goals and ambitions. He will not cheat, betray, or break your trust. He will be understanding and compassionate.

He will be gentle, funny, and the kind of lover that you deserve.

Since, we have already discussed qualities to look for in a man, absolute deal-breakers, and how to set realistic expectations in the previous chapter, consider this a quick yet paramount recap. It will be brief, sweet, and hopeful, aka the perfect combination.

ATTRACTING THE RIGHT MATE

IT'S FUNNY HOW THEY show in documentaries where the female lioness goes for the strongest mate to be her partner. We see at least two lions fighting for her, wanting to claim her. It's all too exciting yet easy.

Real relationships don't work like that. There is more to what a woman wants than just raw masculinity. Real women want to be with real men. They want to be with someone who can make them laugh, be there for them, and allow them to be who they are.

We all look for different things in relationships. Some women seek a sense of security from their partners. Some want love and appreciation. Some are after validation of being good enough because they come from a broken home and never knew what it feels like to have a real family.

No matter what you seek in a romantic exchange, it all starts with finding a man to call yours.

The right man can be just around the corner and yet not see you. He may meet you a hundred times and still not feel that attraction to chase after you. You may come off as too desperate or self-absorbed that he doesn't want to share a life with you.

How you attract the right men is no less than an art in itself. And you, my lady, should master it.

A man of quality seeks the same in his woman. The most basic advice is to become the kind you want to attract. Let go of your self-deprecating thoughts about how you are damaged goods. You are so much more than you think you are. You have so much to offer. Change the way you see yourself.

Be happy. There is nothing more exciting for a man to come across than a woman who has it all. She isn't seeking anything. Whatever she needs, she receives it. She knows how to get it for herself. She is independent, stable, and secure. When she is all that, she becomes a magnet that attracts only the best kind. And the men notice. Oh, they can sense that happy vibe from across the room. Your laughs are genuine. Your stance is confidence. You have poise and you carry yourself with pride. You don't need a man and that is what attracts them the most.

Take good care of yourself. Pamper yourself with affectionate words, shower yourself with gifts and words of gratefulness, and feel wholesome. When you feel good, you ooze confidence. You become irresistible to good men. Learn to invest in yourself.

Be your true authentic self. How would you feel if you fall in love with a man only to find out later that he pretended to be someone else? When you are after an authentic man, you must be authentic yourself. The right man will sense the inconsistent energy that emits from a woman who's faking it. Why would he trade his loaf of bread for something as insignificant as crumbs? By being yourself, you will also weed out the men who aren't interested in the real and genuine you. Your confidence and wholesomeness should radiate from everything you say or do. The more you catch up on the essence of who you are, the better. The right man will see that and wish to be a part of your reality.

Spend time where quality men spend their time. This also depends on who you are seeking. Are you seeking a reader who loves to talk about literature? A library will be a good place to start. If you are looking for a gentleman with refined tastes and artistic qualities, museums and art galleries will help you find him. If you want someone with a kind heart and passion for volunteering, research programs and NGOs that take volunteers in. If you want a guy who shares the same faith as you, a church will do. Although love may happen anytime, anywhere, using some logic to set yourself up to find it won't kill you.

Finally, be hard to get. Men love the thrill of the chase. They put a lot of value on something they have to chase after or compete for. Be someone men would flock around to earn some time with. Don't come off as desperate. Use your charisma, looks, and confidence to charm the kind. Flirt a little but do it with grace. Make them want you in a way they have never wanted another woman.

CONCLUSION

YOU ARE A WOMAN of great prominence. No one but yourself can define your worth and value. You are strong. Something like a heartbreak shouldn't stop you from loving yourself and others again. It doesn't define who you are as a person. It doesn't determine the kind of relationships you will have. Just because something didn't end well doesn't mean that it never will.

Don't underestimate the power you hold. Manifest happiness, peace, and harmony for yourself. If you are healing from a failed relationship, take out the time to self-reflect. Set better standards for the next time. Know what you need from a potential partner, things you won't compromise on, and qualities they must possess.

But before that happens, you need to rediscover your own greatness. You need to mourn and recover. You need to learn how to be assertive and upfront in relationships. You need to know what your expectations are from yourself as a partner. You contribute as much to it as any man you are with. He can make you happy but he isn't responsible for your happiness. You create it for yourself.

Self-love must come before any form of love. Self-compassion and kindness are two things you need to cultivate within yourself. Let go of the idea that a man will do all the things you want for yourself. You do them for yourself. Don't hold back on going on a solo trip because it will be more fun with someone by your side. Don't feel bad about going on a date alone. Your company is the best company there is.

Don't sell yourself short. Just because a past relationship didn't work out the way you wanted it to, it doesn't mean you have to lower your standards for the next one.

Realize your true potential. You are a unique edition, a limited version. Any man would be lucky to have you by his side. Don't forget it is your confidence in yourself and self-esteem that makes you attractive and sexy. Own it and you can attract the man of your dreams while laying down the ground rules for how you want the relationship to proceed.

If that isn't amazing, what is?

Therefore, put in the work. Allow yourself as much time as you need to recover. Don't rush in. Don't do stupid things out of jealousy. You might be tempted to have a rebound relationship but you already know how it isn't healthy. Allow yourself some time to introspect and create a checklist of what qualities you seek in a potential partner.

One day, you will find someone worthy of your time and love. When they come into your life, it will change for the best. I promise!

Thank you for giving this book a read. I hope you enjoyed it as much as I enjoyed writing it. If you picked it up because you felt you needed it, or for someone whom you thought deserved it, let me know how you found it. I would love to hear what you have to say about it.

ALSO BY ELLIE FLORES

Start Loving Again: How to Resolve All Trust Issues, Build Trust in Relationship and Create a Loving Relationship You Deserve (ISBN:978-1955847049)

Relationship After Cheating - A Guide to Recovery from Infidelity, Rebuilding Trust and Moving Forward (ISBN:978-1955847087)

Connecting Love Question Book for Couple: 100 Fun and Thought-Provoking Questions to Strengthen Your Relationship and Rekindle Your Emotional Intimacy (ISBN:978-1955847032)

BONUS BOOK

Something's off about your partner, but you don't know what. Suddenly, they are spending hours in the washroom with their phone, making excuses about their boss keeping them after work hours, sneaking out of the room to take calls late at night, and being uninterested in having sex. Are they conscious about the way they look, upgrading their wardrobe, and hitting the gym? But this isn't like them!

What changed?

Deep down you know... you just don't want to admit it yet.

A cheating partner reveals more through their behavior and actions than through their words. But how to confirm the suspicions, and confront them with evidence?

How to make that confrontation a pivotal point in your relationship where you ask yourself if you want to continue living with the same person? Or leave and move on?

In *How to Discover and Confront Infidelity in Your Relationship*, the author unravels the many warning signs a cheating spouse/partner displays, and also shows how to confirm those doubts. With concrete evidence, let's prepare to have a sensible confrontation, and determine the reasons why your partner cheated...

Download this book for FREE at www.littlebookhut.com

Could You Help

Thank you so much for reading my book and for making it all the way to the end!

I would like to ask you for a small favor. Would you consider sharing your thoughts about my book and post a review on Amazon and Goodreads? Your support means the world to me, as it will help my book gain visibility and attract a wider audience.

Thank you!

Made in the USA
Las Vegas, NV
05 January 2024

83959370R00113